A TR...

CHRISTIAN LOVE

A TREATISE OF

CHRISTIAN LOVE

with an extract from
THE SINNER'S SANCTUARY

Hugh Binning

THE BANNER OF TRUTH TRUST

THE BANNER OF TRUTH TRUST
3 Murrayfield Road, Edinburgh EH12 6EL, UK
P.O. Box 621, Carlisle, PA 17013, USA

*

A Treatise of Christian Love first published 1735
The Sinner's Sanctuary first published 1670
First Banner of Truth edition 2004
ISBN 0 85151 870 2

*

Typeset in 10¹/₂/14 pt Sabon at
the Banner of Truth Trust, Edinburgh
Printed and bound in Great Britain by
Creative Print & Design (Wales)
Ebbw Vale

CONTENTS

Biographical Note[1]

Hugh Binning (1627–53) was born in Dalvennan, Ayrshire, the son of a wealthy landowner. As a young boy he showed a strong aptitude for learning and religious exercises. He graduated from the College of Glasgow in 1646 and soon afterwards, despite his youth, was elected to the chair of Philosophy in the College. Ordained Minister of Govan, near Glasgow, in 1650, he is said to have impressed Oliver Cromwell by the force of his reasoning. In the division of the Scottish Church into Resolutioners and Protesters he took the side of the Protesters, but maintained an irenic spirit and in this context wrote his *Treatise of Christian Love*. He died in 1653 aged only 26.

Though his preaching differed from that of most of his contemporaries in having fewer divisions and sub-divisions, it was warm and practical and gained him great popularity. James Durham said, 'There is no speaking after Mr Binning.' Three sermons from a series of forty on Romans 8:1–15, published in 1670 as *The Sinner's Sanctuary*, are included in this edition. Binning's writings have been deservedly popular, both in the English-speaking world and in the Netherlands, and several of his works have been translated into Dutch.

Some of the language and punctuation of earlier editions have been slightly modernized for this new edition.

[1] Further information on Binning's life can be found in *The Scots Worthies* (ISBN 0 85151 686 6, 672 pp. clothbound).

I

LOVE AND SELF-LOVE

'By this shall all men know that ye are my disciples,
if ye have love one to another' (*John* 13:35).

The beauty and excellency of this world consists, not only in the perfection and comeliness of each part in it, but especially in the wise and wonderful proportion and union of these several parts. It is not the lineaments and colours that make the image, or complete the beauty, but the proportion and harmony of these, though they differ. And truly that is the wonder, that such repugnant natures, such different parts, and dissentient qualities, do conspire together in such an exact, perfect unity and agreement.

In this the wisdom of God most appears, by making all things in number, weight, and measure. His power appears in making all the materials of nothing; but his wisdom is manifested in ordering and disposing dissonant natures into one well-agreeing and comely frame; so that this orderly disposition of all things into one fabric is that harmonious melody of the creation, made up, as it were,

[1]

of dissonant sounds; and that comely beauty of the world, resulting from such a proportion and wise combination of diverse lines and colours. To go no further than the body of a man, what various elements are combined into a well-ordered being, the extreme qualities being so refracted and abated that they may join in friendship and society, and make up one sweet temperament.

Now, it is most reasonable to suppose that, by the law of creation, there was to be no less order and unity among men, the chiefest of the works of God. And so it was indeed: as God had moulded the rest of the world into a beautiful frame by the first stamp of his finger, so he did engrave upon the hearts of men such a principle as might be a perpetual bond and tie to unite the sons of men together. This was nothing else but the law of love, the principal fundamental law of our creation – love to God, founded on our essential dependence on and subordination to God, and love to man, grounded upon that communion and interest in one image of God.

All the commandments of the first and second table are but so many branches of these trees, or streams of these fountains. Therefore, our Saviour gives a complete abridgement of the law of nature and moral law, 'Thou shalt love the Lord thy God, with all thy heart, and with all thy soul, and with all thy mind; this is the first and great commandment: the second is like unto it, Thou shalt love thy neighbour as thyself' (*Matt.* 22:37–39). 'Therefore', as Paul says, 'love is the fulfilling of the law' (*Rom.* 13:10). The universal debt we owe to God is love in the superlative degree; and the universal debt we owe one another is love in an inferior degree, yet of no lower kind than that of ourselves: 'Owe no man anything, but to love one another' (*Rom.* 13:8), and that collateral with himself, as Christ speaks. Unto these laws all others are subordinate, and one of them is subordinate to the other, but to nothing else. And so, as long as the love of God may go before, the love of man should follow; and whatever doth not untie the bond of divine affection ought not to loose the knot of that love which is linked with it. When the uniting of souls together divides both from God, then, indeed, and only then, must this knot be untied, that the other may be kept fast.

But this beautiful and comely frame of man is marred. Sin has cut in pieces that divine love that knit man to God; and the dissolving of this has loosed that link of human society, love to our neighbour. And now all is rents, rags, and distractions, because self-love has usurped the throne. The unity of the world of mankind is dissolved; one is distracted from another, each following their own private inclinations and inordinate affections, which is the poison of enmity, and seed of all discord.

If the love of God and of one another had kept the throne, there had been a co-ordination and co-working of all men in all their actions, for God's glory and the common good of man. But now, self-love having enthroned itself, every man is for himself, and strives by all means, to make a concurrence of all things to his own interest and designs.

The first principles of love would have made all men's actions and courses flow into one ocean of divine glory and mutual edification; so that there could not have been any disturbance or jarring amongst them, all flowing into one common end. But self-love has turned all the channels backward towards itself; and this is its wretched aim and endeavour, in which it wearies itself and discomposes the world, to wind and turn in every thing, and to make, in the end, a general affluence of the streams into its own bosom; this is the seed of all division and confusion which is among men. While every man makes himself the centre, it cannot be otherwise than that all the lines and draughts of men's courses must thwart and cross each other.

Now, the Lord Jesus having redeemed lost man and repaired his ruins, makes up this breach, especially restoring this fundamental ordinance of our creation and uniting men again to God and to one another. Therefore he is our peace; he hath removed the seeds of discord between God and man, and between man and man. And this is the subject of that divine epistle which the beloved apostle, full of that divine love, did pen. 'God is love. In this was manifested the love of God . . . that God sent his only begotten Son into the world'; 'Everyone that loveth is born of God, and knoweth God'; 'We love him, because he loved us first'; 'If God so loved us, we ought also to love one another' (*1 John* 4).

This is the very substance of the gospel, a doctrine of God's love to man, and of man's love due to God, and to them who are begotten of God; the one declared, the other commanded; so that much of the gospel is but a new edition or publication of that ancient fundamental law of creation. This is the paradox which John delivers, 'I write no new commandment unto you, but an old commandment, even that which you had from the beginning. Again, a new commandment I write unto you, which thing is true in him and you; because the darkness is past, and the true light now shineth' (*1 John* 2:7–8).

It is no new commandment, but that primitive command of love to God and men, which is the fulfilling of the law; and yet new it is, because there is a new obligation superadded. The bond of creation was great, but the tie of redemption is greater. God gave a being to man, that is enough; but for God to become a miserable man for man, that is infinitely more.

Fellow-creatures: that is sufficient for a bond of amity; but to be once fellow-captives, companions in misery, and then companions in mercy and blessedness, that is a new and stronger bond. Mutual love was the badge of reasonable creatures in innocency; but now Jesus Christ hath put a new stamp and signification on it, and made it the very differential character and token of his disciples: 'By this shall all men know that ye are my disciples, if ye have love one to another' (*John* 13:35). And therefore when he is making his latter will, he gives this testamentary commandment to his children and heirs, 'A new commandment give I unto you, that ye love one another; as I have loved you, that ye also love one another' (verse 34). New indeed; for though it be the same command, yet there was never such a motive, inducement, and persuasive to it as this: 'God so loved that he gave me, and I so loved that I gave myself'; that is an addition more than all that was before.

There is a special stamp of excellency put on this affection of love, that God delights to exhibit himself to us in such a notion, 'God is love.' And so he holds out himself as the pattern of this, 'Be ye followers of God as dear children, and walk in love' (*Eph.* 5:1–2).

This is the great virtue and property which we should imitate our Father in. God has a general love to all the creatures, from whence the river of his goodness flows out through the earth, and in that it is like the sun conveying his light and benign influence, without partiality or restraint, to the whole world. But his special favour runs in a more narrow channel towards those whom he hath chosen in Christ. So in this a Christian should be like his Father; and there is nothing in which he resembles him more than in this, to walk in love towards all men, even our enemies, for in this he gives us a pattern: 'But I say unto you, love your enemies, bless them that curse you, do good to them that hate you, and pray for them which despitefully use you and persecute you; that ye may be the children of your Father which is in heaven: for he maketh his sun to rise on the evil and on the good, and sendeth rain on the just and on the unjust' (*Matt.* 5:44–45).

To do good to all, and to be ready to forgive all, is the glory of God; and certainly it is the glory of a child of God to be merciful as his Father is merciful, and good to all, and kind to the unthankful; and this is to be perfect as he is perfect. This perfection is charity and love to all.

But the particular and special current of affection will run toward the household of faith; those who are of the same descent, and family, and love. This, drawn into such a compass, is the badge and livery of his disciples. These two in a Christian are nothing but the reflex of the love of God, and streams issuing out from it. A Christian, walking in love to all, blessing his enemies, praying for them; not reviling or cursing again, but rendering blessing for cursing, and praying for reviling; forgiving all, and ready to give to the necessities of all; and more especially, uniting the force of his love and delight, to bestow it upon those who are the excellent ones, and the delight of God: such a one is his Father's picture, so to speak. He is partaker of that divine nature and royal spirit of love. 'As we have therefore opportunity, let us do good unto all men, especially unto them who are of the household of faith' (*Gal.* 6:10). 'And the Lord make you to increase and abound in love one towards another, and towards all men, even as we do towards you: to the end he may stablish your hearts unblameable in holiness before God, even our Father, at the coming of our Lord Jesus Christ, with all his saints' (*1 Thess.* 3:12–13).

It is foretold by our Lord Jesus Christ that, in the last days, 'the love of many shall wax cold' (*Matt.* 24:12). And truly this is the symptom of a decaying and fading Christian and church. Love is the vital spirits of a Christian, the principle of all motion and lively operation.

[7]

When there is a *deliquium* [loss or deficiency] in these, the soul is in a decay.

It is so comprehensive an evil as alone is sufficient to make an evil time; and besides, it is the argument and evidence, as well as the root and fountain, of abounding iniquity. And this is the epidemical disease of the present time, love cooled and passion heated; whence proceed all the feverish distempers, contentions, wars, and divisions which have brought the church of God near to expiring.

Therefore, being mindful of the words of the apostle in Hebrews 10:24, I would think it pertinent to 'consider one another', and 'to provoke again unto love and to good works'.

It was the great charge that Christ had against Ephesus, 'Thou hast left thy first love.' I shall therefore show the excellency and necessity of this grace, that so we may remember from whence we have fallen, and repent, that we may do the first works, lest he come quickly and remove our candlestick (*Rev.* 2:4–5).

2

THE EXCELLENCE OF CHRISTIAN LOVE

Firstly, then, it might endear this Christian virtue unto us that *God proposes himself as the pattern of it, that Christ holds out himself as the rare example of it* for our imitation.

It is what most endears God to creatures, and certainly it must likewise commend them one to another: 'Beloved, let us love one another: for love is of God; and every one that loveth is born of God, and knoweth God. He that loveth not, knoweth not God; for God is love' (*1 John* 4:7–8). 'But I say unto you, Love your enemies, bless them that curse you, do good to them that hate you, and pray for them which despitefully use you, and persecute you: that, you may be the children of your Father which is in heaven, for he maketh his sun to rise on the evil and on the good, and sendeth rain on the just and on the unjust' (*Matt.* 5:44–45). 'Be ye therefore followers of God, as dear children; and walk in love, as Christ also hath loved us, and hath given himself for us, an offering and a sacrifice to God for a sweet-smelling savour' (*Eph*. 5:1–2). 'By this shall all men know that ye are my disciples, if ye have love one to another' (*John* 13:35). Now, the following of so rare an example, and imitating of so noble and high a pattern, exalts the soul into a royalty and dignity, that it dwells in God and God in it (*1 John* 4:16). This is the highest point of conformity with God, and the nearest resemblance to our Father. To be like him in wisdom, that wretched aim did cast men as low as hell; but to aspire unto a likeness in love lifts up the soul as high as heaven, even to a mutual indwelling.

2. It should add an exceeding weight unto it that *we have not only so high a pattern, but so excellent a motive.*
God so loved; and, 'Herein is love, not that we loved God, but that he loved us, and sent his Son to be the propitiation for our sins'; therefore, if God so loved us, we ought also to love one another (*1 John* 4:9–11). 'Walk in love, as Christ also hath loved us, and hath given himself for us' (*Eph*. 5:2). Here are the topics of the most vehement persuasion. There is no invention that can afford so constraining a motive – God so loving us, sinful and miserable us, that he gave his only begotten Son, that we might live through him; and Christ so loving us, that he gave himself a sacrifice for sin. Oh, then, who should live to himself, when Christ died for others? And who should not love, when God spared not his own Son, but delivered him up for us all? 'God commendeth his love toward us,

in that, while we were yet sinners, Christ died for us' (*Rom.* 5:8; see also *Rom.* 8:32; 14:7–8).

3. Join to this *so earnest and pressing a command, even the latter will of him to whom we owe the fact that we are, and are redeemed.*

This is the burden he lays on us; this is all the recompence he seeks for his unparalleled love: 'That ye love one another; as I have loved you, that ye also love one another' (*John* 13:34). 'Your goodness cannot extend to me, therefore I assign all the beneficence and bounty ye owe to me, I give it over to these whom I have loved, and have not loved my life for them; now,' says he, 'whatsoever ye would count yourself obliged to do to me, if I were on the earth among you, do it to these poor ones whom I have left behind me, and this is all the testimony of gratitude I crave.'

'Then shall the King say unto them on his right hand, Come ye blessed of my Father, inherit the kingdom prepared for you from the foundation of the world: For I was an hungred, and ye gave me meat: I was thirsty, and ye gave me drink: I was a stranger, and ye took me in: naked, and ye clothed me: I was sick, and ye visited me: I was in prison, and ye came unto me. Then shall the righteous answer him, saying, Lord, when saw we thee an hungred, and fed thee? or thirsty, and gave thee drink? When saw we thee a stranger, and took thee in? or naked, and clothed thee? Or when saw we thee sick, or in prison, and came unto thee? And the King shall answer, and say unto them, Verily I say unto you, inasmuch as ye have done it unto one of the least of these my brethren, ye have done it unto me' (*Matt.* 25:34–40). 'These ye have always with you, but me ye have not always.'

It is strange, how earnestly, how solicitously, how pungently he presses this exhortation, 'A new commandment I give unto you, that ye love one another; as I have loved you, that ye also love one another. By this shall all men know that ye are my disciples, if ye have love one to another.''This is my commandment, that ye love one another as I have loved you . . . These things I command you, that ye love one another' (*John* 15:12,17).

And his apostles after him: 'But as touching brotherly love, ye need not that I write unto you: for ye yourselves are taught of God to love one another' (*1 Thess.* 4:9); 'And above all these things, put on charity, which is the bond of perfectness' (*Col.* 3:14); 'And above all things have fervent charity among yourselves: for charity shall cover the multitude of sins' (*1 Pet.* 4:8). But above all, that beloved disciple who, being so intimate with Jesus Christ, we may lawfully conceive he was inured to that affectionate frame by his converse with Christ, and has been most mindful of Christ's testamentary injunctions: he cannot speak three sentences, but this is one of them.

All which may convince us of this one thing, that there is a greater moment and weight of Christianity in charity than in the most part of those things for which Christians bite and devour one another. It is the fundamental law of the gospel, to which all positive precepts and ordinances should stoop. Unity in judgment is very needful for the well-being of Christians; but Christ's last words persuade this, that unity in affection is more essential and fundamental; this is the badge he left to his disciples; if we cast away this upon every different apprehension of mind, we disown our Master, and disclaim his token and badge.

4. *The apostle Paul puts a high note of commendation upon charity, when he styles it the bond of perfection.*

'Above all these things', says he, 'put on charity, which is the bond of perfectness' (*Col.* 3:14). I am sure it has not such a high place in the minds and practice of Christians now as it has in the list of the parts and members of the new man here set down. Here it is above all; with us it is below all, even below every apprehension of doubtful truths. An agreement in the conception of any poor, petty controversial matter of the times is made the badge of Christianity, and set in an eminent place above all that the apostle mentions in the twelfth verse, bowels of mercy, kindness, gentleness, humbleness of mind, meekness, long-suffering. Nay, charity itself is but a waiting-handmaid to this mistress.

But let us consider the significant character the apostle puts on it: It is a bond of perfection, as it were, a bundle of graces, and chain of virtues, even the very cream and flower of many graces combined. It is the sweet result of the united force of all graces; it is the very head and heart of the new man, which we are invited to put on: 'Above all, put on charity.' All these fore-mentioned perfections are bound and tied together, by the girdle of charity and love, to the new man.

When charity is born and brought forth, it may be styled Gad, for 'a troop cometh' (*Gen.* 30:11), *chorus virtutum*,[1] a troop or company of virtues which it leads and commands. Charity has a tender heart; for it has bowels of mercies, such a compassionate and melting temper of spirit that the misery or calamity, whether bodily or spiritual, of other men, makes an impression upon it; and, therefore, it is the Christian sympathy which affects itself with others' afflictions. If others be moved, it moves itself through consort and sympathy. This is not only extended to bodily and outward infirmities but, most of all, to infirmities of mind and heart, error, ignorance, darkness, falling and failing in temptation. We are made priests to God our Father, to have compassion on them who are ignorant and out of the way; for that we ourselves are also compassed with infirmity (*Rev.* 1:6; *Heb.* 5:2). Then, love has a humble mind, 'humbleness of mind', else it could not stoop and condescend to others of low degree; and, therefore, Christ exhorts above all to lowliness: 'Learn of me, for I am meek and lowly in heart.' If a man be not lowly, to sit down below offences and infirmities, his love cannot rise above them.

Self-love is the greatest enemy to true Christian love, and pride is the fountain of self-love. Because it is impossible that in this life there should be an exact correspondence between the thoughts and ways of Christians,

[1] This is an allusion to Cicero, *De Officiis*, Book 3, Chap. 33.

therefore it is not possible to keep this bond of perfection unbroken, except there be a mutual condescension. Self-love would have all conformed to it; and if that be not, there is the rent presently; but humbleness of mind can conform itself to all things, and this keeps the bond fast.

Then charity, by the link of humility, has meekness chained to it, and kindness; love is of a sweet complexion, meek and kind. Pride is the mother of passion, humbleness the mother of meekness. The inward affection is composed by meekness, and the outward actions adorned by gentleness and kindness. Oh, that sweet composure of spirit! The heart of the wicked is as the troubled sea; no rest, no quiet in it, continual tempests raising continual waves of disquiet. An unmeek spirit is like a boiling pot: it troubles itself and annoys others. Then, at length, charity, by lowliness and meekness, is the most durable, enduring, long-suffering thing in the world; 'with long-suffering, forbearing one another in love': these are the only principles of patience and forbearance. Anger and passion is expressed in Scripture under the name of haste; and it is a sudden, furious, hasty thing; a rash, inconsiderate, impatient thing; more hasty than speedy. Now the special exercises and operations of these graces are in verse 13, 'Forbearing one another, and forgiving one another,' according to Christ's example; and indeed, these are such high and sublime works that charity must yoke all the forementioned graces, unite them all in one troop, for the accomplishing of them. And the great and sweet fruit of all this is comprehended in verse 15, 'Let the peace of God rule in your hearts, to the which also ye are called in one body.' Peace with God is not here meant, but the peace which God has made up between men. All were shattered and rent asunder; the Lord has by his son Jesus Christ gathered so many into one body, the church; and by one Spirit quickens all. Now, where love is predominant, there is a sweet peace and harmony among all the members of this one body; and this peace and tranquillity of affections rules and predominates over all those lusts, which are the mines of contentions, strifes, and wars.

5. *Add unto this another special mark of excellency, that this apostle puts on Christian love: 'The end of the commandment is charity out of a pure heart, and of a good conscience, and of faith unfeigned' (1 Tim. 1:5).*

If this were duly pondered, I do believe it would fill all hearts with astonishment, and faces with confusion, that they neglected the weightier matters of the law, and over-stretched some other particular duties, to fill up the place of this, which is the end, the fulfilling of the law. It appears by this that charity is a cream of graces; it is the spirit and quintessence extracted out of those cardinal graces, unfeigned faith, a good conscience, a pure heart. It is true, the immediate end of the law, as it is now expounded to us, is to draw us to believe in Jesus Christ, as it is expressed (*Rom.* 10:4), 'Christ is the end of the law for righteousness to every one that believeth.' But this believing in Christ is not the last end of it: faith unfeigned in a Mediator is intentionally for this, to give the answer of a good conscience in the blood of Christ, and to purify the heart by the water of the Spirit; and so to bring about at length, by such a sweet compass, the righteousness of the law to be fulfilled by love in us, which by divine imputation is fulfilled to us.

Now, consider the context, and it shall yield much edification. Some teachers (*1 Tim.* 1:4) exercised themselves and others in endless genealogies, which, though they contain some truth in them, yet they were perplexed, and brought no edification to souls. Curiosity might go round in such debates, and bewilder itself as in a labyrinth; but they did rather multiply disputes than bring true edification in the faith and love of God and man. 'Now,' says he, 'they do wholly mistake the end of the law, of the doctrine of the Scripture'; the end and great purpose of it is love, which proceeds from faith in Christ, purifying the heart. This is the sum of all, to worship God in faith and purity, and to love one another; and whatsoever debates and questions do tend to the breach of this bond, and have no eminent and remarkable advantage in them, suppose they be conceived to be about matters of conscience, yet the entertaining and prosecuting them to the prejudice of this, is a manifest violence offered to the law of God, which is the rule of conscience; it is a perverting of Scripture and conscience to a wrong end.

I say, then, that charity and Christian love should be the moderator of all our actions toward men; from thence they should proceed, and according to this rule be formed. I am persuaded, if this rule were followed, the differences in judgment of godly men, about such matters as minister mere questions, would soon be buried in the gulf of Christian affection.

6. *Now, to complete the account of the eminence of this grace, take that remarkable chapter of Paul's, 1 Corinthians 13, where he institutes the comparison between it and other graces; and in the end pronounces on its behalf, 'The greatest of these is charity.'*

I wonder how we do please ourselves, as if we had attained already, when we do not so much as labour to be acquainted with this, in which the life of Christianity consists: without which faith is dead, our profession vain, our other duties and endeavours for the truth unacceptable to God and man. 'Yet I show you a more excellent way,' says he, in the former chapter; and this is the more excellent way, charity and love, more excellent than gifts, speaking with tongues, prophesying, etc.

And is it not more excellent than the knowledge and acknowledgment of some present questionable matters, about governments, treaties, and such like, and far more than every *punctilio* of them? But he goes higher. Suppose a man could spend all his substance upon the maintenance of such an opinion, and give his life for the defence of it, though in itself it be commendable; yet, if he want charity and love to his brethren, if he overstretch that point of conscience to the breach of Christian affection, and duties flowing from it, it 'profits him nothing'. Then, certainly, charity must rule our external actions, and have the predominant hand in the use of all gifts, in the venting of all opinions. Whatsoever knowledge and ability a man has, charity must employ it and use it; without this, duties and graces make a noise, but they are shallow and empty within. Now he shows the sweet properties of it, and good effects of it: how universal an influence it has on all things, but especially, how necessary it is to keep the unity of the church.

'*Charity is kind*' and '*suffereth long*' [μακροθυμει]; it is longanimous or magnanimous; and there is, indeed, no great, truly great mind, but it is patient and long-suffering. It is a great weakness and meanness of spirit to be soon angry. Such a spirit has not the rule of itself but is in bondage to its own lust. But 'he that ruleth his spirit is better than he that taketh a city'. Now, it is much of this affection of love that over-rules passion: there is a greatness and height in it, to love them that deserve not well of us, to be kind to the unfaithful, not to be easily provoked, and not soon disobliged. A fool's wrath is presently known; it is a folly and weakness of spirit which love, much love, cures and amends. It suffers much unkindness, and *long* suffers it, and yet can be kind.

'*Charity envieth not.*' Envy is the seed of all contention, and self-love brings it forth. When every man desires to be esteemed chief, and would have pre-eminence among others, their ways and courses must interfere one with another. It is this that makes discord. Every man would abate from another's estimation, that he may add to his own. None lives content with his own lot or station, and it is the aspiring beyond that which puts all the wheels out of course. I believe this is the root of many contentions among Christians, the apprehension of slighting, the conceit of disrespect, and such like, kindles the flame of difference, and heightens the least offence to an unpardonable injury. But 'charity envieth not' where it may lie quietly low; though it be under the feet of others, and beneath its own due place, yet it envieth not, it can lie contentedly so. Suppose it is slighted and despised, yet it takes it not highly, because it is 'lowly in mind'.

'*Charity vaunteth not itself, is not puffed up.*' If charity has gifts and graces beyond others, it restrains itself with the bridle of modesty and humility from vaunting or boasting or any thing in its carriage that may savour of conceit. Pride is a self-admirer, and despises others, and to please itself it cares not to displease others. There is nothing so unbearable in human or Christian society, so apt to alienate others' affections, for the more we take of our own affection to ourselves, we shall have the less from others. Oh, these golden rules of Christian walking! 'Be kindly affectioned one to another, with brotherly love, in honour preferring one another.' 'Mind not high things, but condescend to men of low estate. Be not wise in your own conceits' (*Rom.* 12:10,16). Oh, but that were a comely strife among Christians! Each to prefer another in unfeigned love; and 'in lowliness of mind', each to 'esteem another better than himself' (*Phil.* 2:3). 'Knowledge puffeth up', says this apostle (*1 Cor.* 8:1), 'but charity edifieth'. Pride is but a swelling and a tumour of mind, but love is solid piety and real religion.

Then, *'charity doth not behave itself unseemly'* (*1 Cor.* 13:5). Vanity and swelling of mind will certainly break forth into some unseemly action, as vain estimation, and such like; but charity keeps a sweet decorum in all its behaviour, so as not to provoke and irritate others, nor yet to expose itself to contempt or mockery. Or the word may be taken thus, it is *not fastidious*; it accounts not itself disgraced and abused to condescend to men of low estate; it can, with its Master, bow down to wash a disciple's feet, and not think it unseemly. Whatsoever it submits to in doing or suffering, it is not ashamed of it, as if it were not suitable or comely.

'Charity seeketh not her own [things].' Self-denial and true love are inseparable. Self-love makes a monopoly of all things to its own interest, and this is most opposite to Christian affection and communion, which puts all in one bank. If every one of the members should seek its own things, and not the good of the whole body, what a miserable distemper would it cause in the body! We are called into one body in Christ, and, therefore, we should not look on our own things only, 'but every man also on the things of others' (*Phil.* 2:4). There is a public interest of saints' mutual edification in faith and love which

charity will prefer to its own private interest. Addictedness to our own apprehension, and too much self-overweening and self-pleasing, is the grand enemy of that peace to which we are called in one body. Since one Spirit informs and enlivens all the members, what a monstrosity is it for one member to seek its own things, and attend its own private interest only, as if it were a distinct body.

'*Charity is not easily provoked.*' This is the straight and solid firmness of it, that it is not soon moved with external impressions. It is long-suffering, it suffers long and much; it will not be shaken by violent and weighty pressures of injuries; where there is much provocation given, yet it is not provoked. Now, to complete it, it is not easily provoked at light offences. It is strange how little a spark of injuries puts all in a flame, because our spirits are as gunpowder, so capable of combustion through corruption.

How ridiculous, for the most part, are the causes of our wrath! For light things we are heavily moved, and for ridiculous things sadly; even as children who fall out among themselves for toys and trifles, or as beasts that are provoked upon the very show of a colour, as red, or such like. We would save ourselves much labour, if we could judge before we suffer ourselves to be provoked. But now we follow the first appearance of wrong; and being once moved from without, we continue our commotion within, lest we should seem to be angry without a cause. But charity has a more solid foundation. It 'dwells in God, for God is love', and so is truly great, truly high, and looks down with a steadfast countenance upon these lower things. The upper world is continually calm and serene; no clouds, no tempests there, no winds, nothing to disturb the harmonious and uniform motion; but it is this lower world that is troubled and tossed with tempests, and obscured with clouds. So, a soul dwelling in God by love, is exalted above the cloudy region; he is calm, quiet, serene, and is not disturbed or interrupted in his motion of love to God or men.

'Charity thinketh no evil.' Charity is apt to take all things in the best sense. If a thing may be subject to diverse acceptations, it can put the best construction on it. It is so benign and good in its own nature, that it is not inclined to suspect others. It desires to condemn no man, but would gladly, as far as reason and conscience will permit, absolve every man. It is so far from desire of revenge that it is not provoked or troubled with an injury; for that would be nothing else but to wrong itself because others have wronged it already. And it is so far from wronging others that it will not willingly so much as think evil of them.

Yet, if need require, charity can execute justice, and inflict chastisement, not out of desire of another's misery, but out of love and compassion to mankind. *Caritas non punit quia peccatum est, sed ne peccaretur* [Charity does not punish because one has sinned, but so that one should not sin]; it looks more to prevention of future sin than to revenge of a by-past fault; and can do all without any dis-composure of spirit, as a physician cuts a vein without anger. *Quis enim cui medetur irascitur?* Who is angry at his own patient?

'*Charity rejoiceth not in iniquity.*' Charity is not defiled in itself, though it condescends to all. Though it can love and wish well to evil men, yet it rejoices not in iniquity. It is like the sun's light that shines on a dunghill, and is not defiled, receives no tincture from it. Some base and wicked spirits make a sport to do mischief themselves, and take pleasure in others that do it. But charity rejoices in no iniquity or injustice, though it were done to its own enemy. It cannot take pleasure in the unjust sufferings of any who hate it; because it has no enemy but sin and iniquity, and hates nothing else with a perfect hatred.

Therefore, whatever advantage should redound to itself by other men's iniquities, it cannot rejoice that iniquity, its capital enemy, should reign and prevail. But it '*rejoiceth in the truth*'; the advancement and progress of others in the way of truth and holiness is its pleasure; though that should eclipse its own glory, yet it looks not on it with an evil eye. If it can find out any good in them that are enemies to it, it is not grieved to find it and know it, but can rejoice at any thing which may give ground of good construction of them. There is nothing more beautiful in its eyes, than to see every one get his own due, though it alone should come behind.

'*Charity beareth all things.*' By nature we are undaunted heifers, we cannot bear anything patiently; but charity is accustomed to the yoke, to the yoke of reproaches and injuries from others, to a burden of other men's infirmities and failings. We would all be borne upon others' shoulders, but we cannot put our own shoulders under other men's burdens, according to that royal law of Christ (*Rom.* 15:1), 'We then that are strong ought to bear the infirmities of the weak, and not to please ourselves.' And, 'Bear ye one another's burdens, and so fulfil the law of Christ' (*Gal.* 6:2), that is, the law of love, without question.

'*Charity believeth all things.*' Our nature is malignant and wicked, and therefore most suspicious and jealous, and apt to take all in the worst part; but charity has much candour and humanity in it, and can believe well of every man, and believe all things, as far as truth will permit.

It knows that grace can be beside a man's sins; it knows that it itself is subject to similar infirmities; therefore, it is not a rigid and censorious judge; it allows as much latitude *to* others as it would desire *of* others. It is true that it is not blind and ignorant: it is judicious, and has eyes that can discern between colours. *Credit omnia credenda, sperat omnia speranda*; it hopes all things that are hopeful, and believes all things that are believable. If love has not sufficient evidence, yet she believes if there are some probabilities to the contrary, as well as for it; the weight of charity inclines to the better part, and so casts the balance of hope and persuasion; yet being sometimes

[25]

deceived, she has reason to be watchful and wise; for 'the simple believeth every word'.

If charity cannot have ground of believing any good, yet it hopes still: *Qui non est hodie, cras magis aptus erit*,[1] says charity; and therefore it is patient and gentle, waiting on all, 'if peradventure God may give them repentance to the acknowledging of the truth' (*2 Tim*. 2:25). Charity would account it both atheism and blasphemy, to say such a man cannot, will not, find mercy. But to pronounce of such as have been often approved in the conscience of all, and sealed in many hearts, that they will never find mercy, that they have no grace, because of some failings in practice and differences from us, it would not be insobriety, but madness. It is certainly love and indulgence to ourselves that makes us aggravate other men's faults to such a height; self-love looks on other men's failings through a multiplying or magnifying glass; but she puts her own faults behind her back. *Non videt quod in mantica quæ a tergo est*;[2] therefore she can suffer much in herself but nothing in others; and certainly much self-forbearance and indulgence can spare little for others. But charity is just contrary, she is most rigid on her own behalf, will not pardon herself easily; knows no revenge

[1] 'He who is not amenable today, will be more so tomorrow.' This reverses the saying of Ovid, *Qui non est hodie, cras minus aptus erit* (*Remedia Amoris*, ver. 94).

[2] 'She does not see what is in the bag behind her.' This is an allusion to one of Aesop's fables in which Jupiter hangs two bags on men, one on their backs containing their own faults, the other on their chests, containing the faults of others.

but what is spoken of (*2 Cor.* 7:11), self-revenge; and has no indignation but against herself. Thus she can spare much candour and forbearance for others, and has little or no indignation left behind to consume on others.

'*Charity never faileth.*' This is the last note of commendation. Things have their excellency from their use and from their continuance. Both are here. Nothing so useful, no such friend of human or Christian society as charity; the advantage of it reaches all things. But then, it is most permanent and durable. When all shall go, it shall remain; when ordinances, and knowledge attained by means and ordinances, shall vanish, charity shall abide, and then receive its consummation.

Faith of things inevident and obscure shall be drowned in the vision of seeing God's face clearly; hope of things to come shall be exhausted in the possession and fruition of them; but love only remains in its own nature and notion; only it is perfected by the addition of so many degrees as may suit that blessed estate. Therefore, methinks it should be the study of all saints who believe in immortality, and hope for eternal life, to put on that garment of charity, which is the livery of all the inhabitants above. We might have heaven upon earth, as far as is possible, if we dwelt in love, and love dwelt in and possessed our hearts.

What an unsuitable thing might a believer think it, to hate someone in this world whom he must love eternally; and to contend and strive with those, even for matters of small moment, with bitterness and rigidity, with whom he shall have an eternal, uninterrupted unity and fellowship. Should we not be assaying here, how that glorious garment suits us? And truly there is nothing makes a man so heaven-like or God-like as this – much love and charity.

Now there is one further consideration which might persuade us the more to charity, that *here we know but darkly and in part* (1 Cor. 13:9–12), and therefore our knowledge, at best, is but obscure and inevident; often subject to many mistakes and misapprehensions of truth, because of the obscuring glass we are looking through. And therefore, there must be some latitude of love allowed one to another in this state of imperfection, else it is impossible to keep unity; and we must conflict often with our own shadows, and bite and devour one another for some deceiving appearances.

The imperfection and obscurity of knowledge should make all men jealous of themselves, especially in matters of a doubtful nature, and not so clearly determined by Scripture. Because our knowledge is weak, shall our love be none? Nay, rather let charity grow stronger, and aspire unto perfection, just because knowledge is imperfect. What is wanting in knowledge, let us make up in affection; and let the gap of difference in judgment be swallowed up with the bowels of mercies, love, and humbleness of mind. And then we shall have hid our infirmity of understanding as much as may be. Thus we may go hand in hand together to our Father's house, where, at length, we must be together.

3

MOTIVES TO CHRISTIAN LOVE

I may briefly reduce the chief persuading motives to this so needful and so desirable grace into some three or four heads. All things within and without persuade to it; but especially the right consideration of *the love of God in Christ*, the wise and the impartial reflection on *ourselves*, the consideration of *our brethren whom we are commanded to love*, and a thorough inspection into *the nature and use of the grace itself.*

1. THE LOVE OF GOD IN CHRIST

In consideration of the first, a soul might argue itself into a complacency with it, and thus persuade itself: ' He that loveth not, knoweth not God, for God is love' (*1 John* 4:8). And since he that has known and believed the love that God has to us must certainly 'dwell in love', since these two have such a strict, indissoluble connection, then, as I would not declare to all my atheism and my ignorance of God, I will study to love my brethren; and that I may love them, I will give myself to the search of God's love, which is the place, *locus inventionis*,[1] whence I may find out the strongest and most effectual *medium* to persuade my mind and to constrain my heart to Christian affection.

i. First, then, when I consider that so glorious and so great a Majesty, so high and holy a One, self-sufficient and all-sufficient, who need not go abroad to seek delight, because all happiness and delight is inclosed within his own bosom; yet that he can love a creature, yea, and be reconciled to so sinful a creature, which he might crush as easily as speak a word; that he can place his delight on so unworthy and base an object, oh, how much more should I, a poor wretched creature, love my fellow-creature, ofttimes better than myself, and, for the most part, not much worse!

There is an infinite distance and disproportion between God and man; yet he came over all that to love man. What difficulty should I have, then, to place my affection on my equal at worst, and often better? There cannot be any proportionable distance between the highest and lowest, between the richest and poorest, between the most wise and the most ignorant, between the most gracious and the most ungodly, as there is between the infinite God

[1] *Locus inventionis* and *medium* are logical terms. The former was the starting point of an argument and the latter the middle term.

and a finite angel. Should, then, the mutual infirmities and failings of Christians be an insuperable and impassable gulf, as between heaven and hell, that none can pass over by a bridge of love to either? If God so loved us, should not we love one another (*1 John* 4:11)? And besides, when I consider that God has not only loved me but my brethren, who were worthy of hatred, with an everlasting love, and passed over all that was in them, and has 'spread his skirt over their nakedness, and made it a time of love', which was a time of loathing; how can I withhold my affection where God has bestowed his? Are they not infinitely more unworthy of his than mine? Since infinite wrongs have not changed his, shall poor, petty, and light offences, hinder mine? That my love concentre with God's on the same persons, is it not enough?

ii. Next, that Jesus Christ, 'the only begotten of the Father, full of grace and truth', who was the Father's delight from eternity, and in whom he delighted, yet, notwithstanding, could 'rejoice in the habitable places of the earth' and so love poor wretched men, 'yet enemies' that he gave himself for them; that God so loved that he gave his Son, and Christ so loved that he gave himself a sacrifice for sin, both for me and others; oh, who should not, or will not be constrained, in beholding this mirror of incomparable and spotless love, to love others? 'In this was manifested the love of God towards us, because that God sent his only begotten into the world, that we might live through him. Herein is love, not that we loved God, but that he loved us, and sent his Son to be the propitiation for our sins. Beloved, if God so loved us, we ought also to love one another' (*1 John* 4:9–11). 'And walk in love, as Christ also has loved us, and hath given himself for us, an offering and a sacrifice to God for a sweet-smelling savour' (*Eph.* 5:2), especially when he seems to require no other thing, and imposes no more grievous command upon us for recompense of all his labour of love. 'A new commandment I give unto you, that ye love one another; as I have loved you, that ye also love one another. By this shall all men know that ye are my disciples, if ye have love one to another' (*John* 13:34–35).

If all that was in me did not alienate his love from me, how should any thing in others estrange our love to them? If God be so kind to his enemies, and Christ so loving that he gives his life for his enemies to make them friends, what should we do to our enemies, what to our friends? This one example may make all created love to blush and be ashamed. How narrow, how limited, how selfish it is!

iii. Thirdly, if God has forgiven me so many grievous offences, if he has pardoned so heinous and innumerable injuries that amount to a kind of infinity in number and quality, oh, how much more am I bound to forgive my brethren a few light and trivial offences! *Col.* 3:13: 'Forbearing one another, and forgiving one another; if any man have a quarrel against any, even as Christ forgave you, so also do ye.' *Eph.* 4:32: 'And be ye kind one to another, tender-hearted, forgiving one another, even as God for Christ's sake hath forgiven you.' With what face can I pray, 'Lord, forgive me my sins', when I may meet with such a retort as, 'Thou canst not forgive thy brethren's sins, infinitely less both in number and degree.' *Matt.* 6:15: 'But if ye forgive not men their trespasses, neither will your heavenly Father forgive your trespasses.'

What unparalleled ingratitude would it be, what monstrous wickedness, that after he has forgiven all our debt, because we desired him, yet we should not have compassion on our fellow-servants, even as he had pity on us! Oh, what a dreadful sound will that be in the ears of many Christians! 'O thou wicked servant, I forgave thee all thy debt, because thou desiredst me. Shouldest not thou also have had compassion on thy fellow-servant, even as I had pity on thee? And his lord was wroth, and delivered him to the tormentors, till he should pay all that was due unto him. So likewise shall my heavenly Father do also unto you if ye from your hearts forgive not every one his brother their trespasses' (*Matt.* 18:32–35).

When we cannot dispense with our pence, how should he dispense with his talents? And when we cannot pardon ten, how should he forgive ten thousand? When he has forgiven my brother all his iniquity, may not I pardon one? Shall I impute that which God will not impute; or discover that which God has covered? How should I expect he should be merciful to me, when I cannot show mercy to my brother. *Psa.* 18:25: 'With the merciful thou wilt show thyself merciful.' Shall I, for one or few offences, hate, bite, and devour him for whom Christ died, and loved not his life to save him (*Rom.* 14:15; 1 *Cor.* 8:11)?

2. OURSELVES

i. In the next place, if a Christian do but take an impartial view of himself, he cannot but thus reason himself to a meek, composed, and affectionate temper towards other brethren:

What is it in another that offends me, which, if I do search within, I will not either find the same, or worse, or as evil in myself? Is there 'a mote in my brother's eye'? Perhaps there may be a beam in my own; and why then should I look to the mote that is in my brother's eye (*Matt.* 7:3)? When I look inwardly, I find a 'desperately wicked heart', which lodges all that iniquity I beheld in others. And if I be not so sensible of it, it is because it is also deceitful above all things, and would flatter me in mine own eyes (*Jer.* 17:9). If my brother offends me in some things, how do these vanish out of sight in the view of my own guiltiness before God, and of the abominations of my own heart, known to his holiness and to my conscience? Sure, I cannot see so much evil in my brother as I find in myself; I see but his outside, but I know my own heart; and whenever I retire within this, I find the sea of corruption so great, that I wonder not at the streams which break forth in others; but all my wonder is that God has set bounds to it in me or in any. Whenever I find my spirit rising against the infirmities of others, and my mind swelling over them, I repress myself with this thought, 'I myself also am a man', as Peter said to Cornelius when he would have worshipped him. As he restrained another's idolizing of him, I may cure my own self-idolizing heart. Is it anything strange that weak men fail, and sinful men fall? Is not all flesh grass, and all the perfection and goodliness of it as the flower of the field (*Isa.* 40:6)? Is not every man at his best estate altogether vanity (*Psa.* 39:5)? Is not man's breath in his nostrils (*Isa.* 2:22)? And am not I myself a man? Therefore I will not be high-minded but fear (*Rom.* 11:2). I will not be moved to indignation, but provoked to compassion, knowing that I myself am compassed with infirmities (*Heb.* 5:2).

ii. Secondly, as a man may persuade himself to charity by the examination of his own heart and ways, so he may enforce upon his spirit a meek and compassionate stamp by the consideration of his own frailty, what he may fall into. This is the apostle's rule (*Gal.* 6:1), 'Brethren, if a man be overtaken in a fault, ye that are spiritual', and pretend to it, 'restore such an one in the spirit of meekness.' Do not please yourselves with a false notion of zeal, thinking to cover your impertinent rigidity by it; do as you would do if your own arm were disjointed: set it in, restore it tenderly and meekly, 'considering thyself, lest thou also be tempted'.

Some are more given to reproaching and insulting than mindful of restoring. Therefore, their reproofs are not tempered with oil, that they may not break the head; but mixed with gall and vinegar to set the teeth on edge. But whenever thou lookest upon the infirmities of others, then consider thyself first, before thou pronounce sentence on them, and thou shalt be constrained to bestow that charity to others which thou hast need of thyself. *Veniam petimusque damusque vicissim.*[1] If a man have need of charity from his brother, let him not be hard in giving it; if he know his own weakness and frailty, surely he may suppose such a thing may likely fall out, that he may be tempted and succumb in it; for there needs nothing for the bringing forth of sin in any but occasion and temptation, as the bringing of fire near gunpowder. And truly, he who has no allowance of love to give to an infirm and weak brother, he will be *in mala fide*, in an evil capacity, to seek what he would not give.

Now the fountain of uncharitable and harsh dealing is indicated in Galatians 6:3, 'If a man think himself to be something, when he is nothing, he deceiveth himself.' Since all mortal men are nothing, vanity, altogether vanity, and less than vanity, he that would seem something, and seems so to himself, he deludes himself. Hence is our insulting fierceness, hence our supercilious rigour; every man apprehends some excellency in himself beyond another. Take away pride, and charity shall enter, and modesty shall be its companion. But now we mock ourselves, and deceive ourselves, by building the weight of

---

[1] 'We both seek this indulgence and grant it in turn.' This is a quotation from Horace, *De Arte Poetica*, ver. 11.

our pretended zeal upon such a vain and rotten foundation as a gross, practical, fundamental lie of self-conceit, of a conceit of nothing. Now the apostle furnishes us with an excellent remedy against this in the fourth verse, 'Let every man prove his own work, and then shall he have rejoicing in himself alone, and not in another', a word worthy to be fastened by the Master of assemblies in the heart of all Christians; and indeed this nail driven in would drive out all conceit. Hence is our ruin, that we 'compare ourselves among ourselves', and in so doing we 'are not wise' (2 Cor. 10:12). For we know not our own true value, only we raise the price according to the market, so to speak; we measure ourselves by another man's measure, and build up our estimation upon the disesteem of others; and how much others displease, so much we please ourselves.

'But', says the apostle, 'let every man prove his own work', search his own conscience, compare himself to the perfect rule; and then, if he find all well, he may indeed glory of himself. But that which thou hast by comparison with others is not thine own; thou must come down from all such advantages of ground, if thou wouldst have thy just measure. And indeed, if thou prove thyself and thy work after this manner, thou wilt be the first to reprove thyself, thou shalt have that glory due to thee, that is, none at all; for 'every man shall bear his own burden', when he appears before the judgment-seat of God. There is no place for such imaginations and comparisons in the Lord's judgment.

iii. Thirdly, when a Christian looks within his own heart he finds an inclination and desire to have the love of others, even though his conscience witnesses that he deserves it not; he finds an approbation of that good and righteous command of God, that others should love him. Now hence he may persuade himself, Is it so sweet and pleasant to me to be loved of others, even though I am conscious that I have wronged them? Has it such a beauty in my eye, while I am the object of it? Why then should it be a hard and grievous burden to me to love others, though they have wronged me, and deserve it no more than I did? Why has it not the same amiable aspect, when my brother is the object of it? Certainly no reason for it, but because I am yet carnal, and have not that fundamental law of nature yet distinctly written again upon my heart, 'Whatsoever ye would that men should do to you, do ye even so to them' (*Matt.* 7:12).

If I be convinced that there is any equity and beauty in that command which charges others to love me, forgive me, forbear with me, and restore me in meekness, why, then, should it be a grievous command that I should pay that debt of love and tenderness to others? *1 John* 5:3: 'For this is the love of God, that we keep his commandments: and his commandments are not grievous.'

3. THE OBJECTS OF CHRISTIAN LOVE

In the third place, consider to whom this affection should be extended; more generally to all men, as fellow-creatures: but particularly and especially to all who are

begotten of God, as fellow-Christians. 'And this commandment have we from him, that he who loveth God,
love his brother also. Whosoever believeth that Jesus is
the Christ is born of God: and every one that loveth him
that begat loveth him also that is begotten of him' (*1 John*
4: 21; 5:1). 'As we have therefore opportunity, let us do
good unto all men, especially unto them who are of the
household of faith' (*Gal.* 6:10). 'O my soul, thou hast said
unto the LORD, thou art my Lord: my goodness extendeth
not to thee; but to the saints that are in the earth, and to
the excellent in whom is all my delight' (*Psa.* 16:2–3).

And this consideration the Holy Ghost suggests to make
us maintain love and unity. Love towards these runs in a
purer channel, 'Seeing ye have purified your souls in obey-
ing the truth through the Spirit, unto unfeigned love of
the brethren, see that ye love one another, with a pure
heart fervently: being born again, not of corruptible seed,
but of incorruptible, by the word of God which liveth and
abideth for ever' (*1 Pet.* 1:22–23). To be begotten of one
Father, and that by a divine birth, that they have such a
high descent and royal generation; there are so many
other bonds of unity between us, it is absurd that this one
more should not join all. One Lord, one faith, one bap-
tism, one body, one spirit, called to one hope, one God
and Father of all (*Eph.* 4:2–6). All these being one, it is
strange if we be not one in love. If so many relations
beget not a strong and warm affection, we are worse than
infidels, as the apostle speaks (*1 Tim.* 5:8): 'If any provide
not for his own', his worldly interests, 'he . . . is worse

than an infidel'; for they have a natural affection. Sure then this more excellent nature, a divine nature, which we are partakers of, cannot want affection suitable to its nature. Christianity is a fraternity, a brotherhood, that should overpower all relations, bring down him of high degree, and exalt him of low degree: it should level all ranks, in this one respect, unto the rule of charity and love. In Christ there is neither Jew nor Gentile; there all differences of tongues and nations are drowned in this interest in Christ (*Col.* 3:11). 'Thou hast hid these things from the wise and prudent, and revealed them unto babes' (*Luke* 10:21). And God hath chosen the weak and foolish to confound the mighty and wise (*1 Cor.* 1:27).

Behold all these outward privileges buried in the depths and riches of God's grace and mercy! Are we not all called to one high calling? Our common station is to war under Christ's banner against sin and Satan. Why, then, do we leave our station, forget our callings, and neglect that employment which concerns us all; and fall at odds with our fellow-soldiers, and bite and devour one another? Doth not this give advantage to our common enemies? While we consume the edge of our zeal and strength of our spirits one upon another, they must needs be blunted and weakened towards our deadly enemies. If our brother be represented unto us under the covering of many faults, failings, and obstinacy in his errors, or such like; if we can behold nothing but spots on his outside, while we judge after some outward appearance; then I say, we ought to consider him again under another notion and relation, as he stands in Christ's account; as he is radically and virtually of that seed which has more real worth in it than all worldly privileges and dignities.

Consider him as he once shall be, when mortality shall be put off; learn to strip him naked of all infirmities in thy consideration, and imagine him to be clothed with immortality and glory; and think how thou wouldest then love him. If either thou unclothe him of his infirmities, and consider him as vested now with the robe of Christ's righteousness, and 'all glorious within', or adorned with immortality and incorruption a little hence; or else, if thou clothe thyself with such infirmities as thou seest in him, and consider that thou art not less subject to failing, and 'compassed with infirmity', then thou shalt put on, and keep on, that 'bond of perfection, charity'.

4. The Nature of This Grace

Let us consider the excellent nature of charity; and how it is interested in, and interwoven with, all the royal and divine gifts and privileges of a Christian. None of them are ashamed of kindred and family relation with charity. Is not the calling and profession of a Christian honourable? Sure, to any believing soul, it is above a monarchy, for it includes an anointing both to a royal and priestly office, and carries a title to a kingdom 'incorruptible and undefiled'. Well, then, charity is the symbol and badge of this profession (*John* 13:35), 'By this shall all men know that ye are my disciples, if ye have love one to another.' Then, what is comparable to communion with God, and dwelling in him? 'Shall God indeed dwell with men?', said Solomon. That exalts the soul to a royalty, and elevates it above mortality. *Quam contempta res est homo si supra humana se non exerat*; how base and contemptible a thing is man, except he lift up his head above human things to heavenly and divine things! And then is the soul truly magnified while it is ascending up to its own element, a divine nature.

What more gracious than this, for a soul to 'dwell in God'? And what more glorious than this, God to dwell in the soul? *Caritas te domum Domini facit, et Dominum domum tibi; felix adifex caritas quae conditori sui domum fabricare potest*; love makes the soul a house for the Lord, and makes the Lord a house to the soul; happy artificer that can build an house for its master. Love brings him, who is 'the chief among ten thousand', into the chambers of the heart, it 'lays [him] all night between its breasts' (see *Song of Sol.* 1:13); and is still emptying itself of 'all superfluity of naughtiness', and purging out all vanity and filthiness, that there may be more room for his Majesty.

And then, love 'dwells in God', in his love and grace, in his goodness and greatness, the secret of his presence it delights in. Now, this mutual inhabitation, in which it is hard to say whether the majesty of God does most descend, or the soul most ascend, whether he be more humbled or it exalted, this brotherly love, I say, is the evidence and assurance of it. 'If we love one another, God dwells in us, and his love is perfected in us . . . God is love; and he that dwelleth in love dwelleth in God, and God in him' (*1 John* 4:12, 16). For the love of the image of God in his children is indeed the love of God, whose image it is; and then is the love of God perfected, when it reaches and extends from God to all that is God's, to all that has interest in God: *His commandments* (*1 John* 5:3), 'This is the love of God, that we keep his commandments, and his commandments are not grievous.' *1 John* 4:21: 'And this commandment have we from him, That he who loveth God love his brother also.' *His children* (*1 John* 5:1), 'Whosoever believeth that Jesus is the Christ is born of God, and every one that loveth him that begat, loveth him that is begotten of him.' *His creatures* (*Mal.* 2:10), 'Hath not one God created us? why do we deal treacherously every man against his brother?'

The love of God being the formal, the special motive of love to our brethren, it elevates the nature of it, and makes it divine love; he that has true Christian love, does not only love and have compassion on his brother, either because of his own inclination towards him, or because of his brother's misery and necessity, or goodness and excellency; these motives and grounds do not transcend mere morality, and so cannot beget a love which is the symptom of Christianity. If there be no other motives than these, we do not love so much for God as for ourselves; for compassion interesting itself in another's misery finds a kind of relief in relieving it; therefore, the will and good pleasure of God must be the rule of this motion, and the love of God must begin it, and continue it. And truly, charity is nothing else but divine love in a state of condescension, so to speak, or the love of a soul to God manifested in the flesh; it is that love moving in a circle from God towards his creatures and unto God again; as his love to the creatures begins in himself, and ends in himself (1 John 3:17).

Is it not a high thing to know God aright? 'This is life eternal, to know thee, the only true God, and Jesus Christ whom thou hast sent' (John 17:3). That is a high note of excellency put on it, this makes the face of the soul to shine; now, brotherly love evinceth this, that we know God. 'Beloved, let us love one another: for love is of God; and every one that loveth is born of God, and knoweth God. He that loveth not, knoweth not God, for God is love' (1 John 4:7-8). Love is real light, light and life, light and heat both. 'Did not thy father . . . do judgment and justice . . . was not this to know me? saith the LORD (Jer. 22:15-16). The practice of the most common things, out of the love of God, and respect to his commands, is more real and true religion than the most profound and abstracted speculations of knowledge; then only is God known, when knowledge stamps the heart with fear and reverence of his Majesty, and love to his name; because then only is he known as a true and living God.

Love is real light and life. Is it not a pleasant thing for the eye to behold the sun? Light is sweet, and life is precious, these are two of the rarest jewels given to man. Now, 'he that saith he is in the light, and hateth his brother, is in darkness even until now . . . and knoweth not whither he goeth, because that darkness hath blinded his eyes'; but 'he that loveth his brother abideth in the light, and there is none occasion of stumbling in him' (*1 John* 2:9–11). 'We know that we have passed from death unto life, because we love the brethren. He that loveth not his brother abideth in death' (*1 John* 3:14).

The light of Jesus Christ cannot shine into the heart but it begets love, even as intense light begets heat: and where this impression is not made on the heart, it is an evidence that the beams of that Sun of righteousness have not pierced it. Oh, how suitable it is for a child of light to walk in love! And wherefore is it made day-light to the soul, but that it may rise up and go forth to labour, and exercise itself in the works of the day, duties of love to God and men? Now, in such a soul there is no cause of stumbling, no scandal, no offence in its way to fall over. When the light and knowledge of Christ possess the heart in love there is no stumbling-block of transgression in its way. It does not fall and stumble at the commandments of righteousness and mercy as grievous. 'Therefore love is the fulfilling of the law' (*Rom.* 13:10).

And so, the way of charity is the most easy, plain, expedient, and safe way; in this way, there is light shining all along it, and there is no stumbling-block in it: for the love of God and of our brethren has polished and made it all plain, has taken away the asperities and swellings of our affections and lusts. *Complanavit affectus*, love has levelled. 'Great peace have all they that love thy law, and nothing shall offend them.' Love makes an equable and constant motion; it moves swiftly and sweetly; it can loose many knots without difficulty, which other more violent principles cannot cut; it can melt away mountains before it, which cannot be hurled away.

Albeit there be many stumbling-blocks without in the world, yet there is none in charity, or in a charitable soul: none can enter into that soul to hinder it to possess itself in meekness and patience; nothing can discompose it within, or hinder it to live peaceably with others; though all men's hands be against it, yet charity is against none, it defends itself with innocence and patience. On the other hand, 'He that hateth his brother is in darkness, even until now'; for if Christ's light had entered, then the love of Christ would have come with it, and that is the law of love and charity. If Jesus Christ had come into the soul, he would have restored the ancient commandment of love, and made it new again; as much of the want of love and charity, so much of the old ignorance and darkness remains.

Whatsoever a man may fancy of himself, that he is in the light, that he is so much advanced in the light; yet certainly, this is a stronger evidence of remaining darkness; for it is a work of the darkest darkness, and murdering affection, suitable only for the night of darkness. And such a man, he knows not whither he goes, and must needs incur and fall upon many stumbling-blocks within and without. It is want of love and charity that blinds the mind and darkens the heart, so that it cannot see how to eschew and pass by scandals in others, but it must needs dash and break its neck upon them. Love is a light which may lead us by offences inoffensively, and without stumbling. In darkness men mistake the way, know not the end of it, take pits for plain ways, and stumble in them. Uncharitableness casts a mist over the actions and courses of others, and our own too, so that we cannot carry on either without transgression. And this is the misery of it, that it cannot discern any fault in itself, it knows not whither it goeth, calls light darkness, and darkness light; it is partial in judgment, pronounces always on its own behalf, cares not whom it condemns, that it may absolve itself.

Is there any privilege so precious as this, to be the sons of God (*1 John* 3:2)? What are all relations, or states, or conditions to this one, to be the children of the Highest? It was David's question, 'Should I be the king's son-in-law?' Alas! what a petty and poor dignity compared with this, to be the sons of God, partakers of a divine nature! All the difference of birth, all the distinction of degrees and qualities amongst persons, beside this one, are but such as have no being, no worth but in the fancy, and construction of them, they are really nothing, and can do nothing; this only is a substantial and fundamental difference.

A divine birth carries along with it a divine nature; a change of principles, from the worst to the best, from darkness to light, from death to life. Now, imagine, then, what excellency is in this grace, which is made the character of a son of God, of one begotten of the Father, and passed from death to life. *1 John* 3:10–14: 'In this the children of God are manifest, and the children of the devil: whosoever doeth not righteousness is not of God, neither he that loveth not his brother. We know that we have passed from death unto life, because we love the brethren: he that loveth not his brother abideth in death.' *1 John* 4:7: 'Beloved, let us love one another: for love is of God; and every one that loveth is born of God, and knoweth God.'

And truly, it is most natural if it be so, that the children of our Father love each other dearly; it is monstrous and unnatural to see it otherwise. But besides, there is in this a great deal of resemblance of their Father, whose eminent and signal property it is, to be good to all, and kind even to the unthankful; and whose incomparable glory it is to pardon iniquity, and suffer long patiently. A Christian cannot resemble his Father more nearly than in this. Why do we account that baseness in us which is glory to God? Are we ashamed of our birth, or dare we not own our Father? Shall we be ashamed to love those as brethren whom he has not been ashamed to adopt as sons, and whom Christ is not ashamed to call brethren?

4

CHRISTIAN LOVE IN PRACTICE

We shall not be curious in the ranking of the duties in which Christian love should exercise itself: all the commandments of the second table are but branches of it; they might all be reduced to the works of *righteousness* and of *mercy*. But truly, these are interwoven through each other. Though mercy is usually restricted to the showing of compassion upon men in misery, yet there is a righteousness in that mercy; and there is mercy in most acts of righteousness, as in not judging rashly, in forgiving, etc.; therefore, we shall consider the most eminent and difficult duties of love which the Word of God solemnly and frequently charges upon us in relation to others, especially those of the household of faith.

1. I conceive we would labour to enforce upon our hearts, and persuade our souls to, *a love of all men* by often ruminating upon the words of the apostle which

enjoin us to 'abound in love . . . toward all men' (*1 Thess.* 3:12), and this is so much his concern that he prays earnestly that the Lord would make them increase in it; and this we should pray for too.

An affectionate disposition towards our common nature is not a common thing. Christianity enjoins it, and it is only true humanity (*Luke* 6:36–37), 'Be ye therefore merciful, as your Father also is merciful. Judge not, and ye shall not be judged: condemn not, and ye shall not be condemned: forgive, and ye shall be forgiven.' Now, in relation to all men, charity has an engagement upon it to pray for all sorts of men, from that apostolic command (*1 Tim.* 2:1), 'I exhort, therefore, that, first of all, supplications, prayers, intercessions, and giving of thanks, be made for all men.' Prayers and supplications, earnest prayers out of affection, should be poured out, even for them that cannot, or do not, pray for themselves. Why are we taught to pray, but that we may be the mouth of others?

And since an Intercessor is given to us above, how are we bound to be intercessors for others below; and so to be affected with the common mercies of the multitude as to give thanks too! If man, by the law of creation, is the mouth of the stones, trees, birds, beasts, of heaven and earth, sun, moon, and stars, how much more ought a Christian, a redeemed man, to be the mouth of mankind, to praise God for the abounding of his goodness, even towards those who are left yet in that misery and bondage that he is delivered from?

2. Next, *charity by all means will avoid offence, and live honestly in the sight of all men.* 'Give none offence, neither to the Jews, nor to the Gentiles, nor to the church of God' (*1 Cor.* 10:32). And he adds his own example: 'Even as I please all men in all things, not seeking mine own profit, but the profit of many, that they may be saved' (verse 33).

Charity is not self-addicted; it has no humour to please, it can displease itself to profit others. I do verily think there is no point of Christianity less regarded. Others we acknowledge, but we fail in practice; this scarce has the approbation of the mind; few do conceive an obligation lying on them to it. But oh, how is Christianity, the most of it, humanity! Christ makes us men as well as Christians. He makes us reasonable men when believers. Sin transformed our nature into a wild, beastly, viperous, selfish thing; grace restores reason and natural affection in the purest and highest strain. And this is reason and humanity elevated and purified, to condescend to all men in all things for their profit and edification, to deny one-self to save others.

Whatsoever is not necessary in itself, we ought not to impose a necessity upon it by our imagination and fancy, to the prejudice of a greater necessity – another's edification. Indeed, charity will not, dare not, sin to please men; that were to hate God, to hate ourselves, and to hate our brethren under a base pretended notion of love. But, I believe, addictedness to our own humours in things not necessary, which have no worth but from our disposition,

[51]

does oftener transport us beyond the bounds of charity than the apprehension of duty and conscience of sin. Some will grant they should be tender of offending the saints; but they do not conceive it is very important what they do in relation to others, as if it were lawful to murder a Gentile more than a Christian. That is a bloody imagination opposite to that innocent Christian, Paul (*Phil.* 2:15): 'That ye may be blameless and harmless, the sons of God, without rebuke, in the midst of a crooked and perverse generation, among whom ye shine as lights in the world.' And truly it is humanity, elevated by Christianity, or reason purified by religion, that is the light that shines most brightly in this dark world (*Col.* 4:5): 'Walk in wisdom toward them that are without'; and,'Walk honestly toward them that are without' (*1 Thess.* 4:12), avoiding all things, in our profession and carriage, which may alienate them from the love of the truth and godliness; walking so as we may insinuate into their hearts some apprehension of the beauty of religion.

Many imagine that if they do good all is well; if it be a duty, giving offence matters nothing. But remember that caution, 'Let not then your good be evil spoken of' (*Rom.* 14:16). We would have our eyes upon that too, so to circumstantiate all our duties as they may have least offence in them, and be exposed to least obloquy of men (*1 Pet.* 2:12), 'Having your conversation honest among the Gentiles: that, whereas they speak against you as evildoers, they may by your good works, which they shall behold, glorify God in the day of visitation.'

3. Then, thirdly, *charity 'follows peace with all men', as much as is possible* (*Heb*. 12:14). 'If it be possible, as much as lieth in you, live peaceably with all men' (*Rom*. 12:18). Many spirits are framed for contention; if peace follow them, they will flee from it. But a Christian, having made peace with God, the sweet fruit of that upon his spirit is to dispose him to a peaceable and quiet condescendency to others; and if peace flee from him, to follow after it, not only to entertain it when it is offered, but to seek it when it is away, and to pursue it when it runs away (*Psa*. 34:14); which Peter urges upon Christians (*1 Pet*. 3:8–11), 'Finally, be ye all of one mind, having compassion one of another; love as brethren, be pitiful, be courteous: not rendering evil for evil, or railing for railing: but contrariwise blessing; knowing that ye are thereunto called, that ye should inherit a blessing. For he that will love life, and see good days, let him refrain his tongue from evil, and his lips that they speak no guile: let him eschew evil, and do good; let him seek peace, and ensue it.'

I think that, since we obtained the mercy to get a peacemaker between us and God, we should henceforth count ourselves bound to be peace-makers among men. And truly, such have a blessing pronounced upon them (*Matt*. 5:9), 'Blessed are the peace-makers.' The Prince of Peace pronounced it, and this is the blessedness, 'They shall be called the children of God'; because he is the God of peace, and to resemble him in these, first in purity, then in peace, is a character of his image. It is true, peace will sometimes flee so fast, and so far away, that a Christian cannot follow it without sin, and that is a breach of a higher peace. But charity, when it cannot live in peace without, it does then live in peace within, because it has that sweet testimony of conscience that, as far as did lie in it, peace was followed without. Divine wisdom (*James* 3:17), 'is first pure, then peaceable, gentle, and easy to be intreated, full of mercy and good fruits, without partiality, and without hypocrisy.'

If wisdom is peaceable and not pure, it is but a carnal conspiracy in iniquity, earthly and sensual; but if it is pure, it must be peaceable; for the wisdom descending from above has a purity of truth, and a purity of love, and a purity of the mind and of the affection too. Where there is a purity of truth, but accompanied with envying, bitter strife, rigid judging, wrangling, and such like; then it is defiled, and corrupted by the intermixture of vile and base affections, ascending out of the dunghill of the flesh. The vapours of our lusts, rising up to the mind, do coarsen pure truth. They put an earthly, sensual, and devilish visage on it.

4. *Charity, in its conversation and discourse, is without judging, without censuring;* see Matthew chapter 7, of which chapter, because it contains much edification, I shall speak more hereafter. *James* 3:17: 'Without partiality, without hypocrisy.' The words in the original are αδιακριτος και ανυποκριτος, without judging and wrangling, and without hypocrisy; showing that great

censurers are often the greatest hypocrites, and sincerity has always much charity. Truly, there is much idle time spent this way in discourses of one another, and venting our judgments of others. As if it were enough of commendation for us to condemn others, and much piety to charge another with impiety. We would even be sparing in judging them that are without (*1 Cor.* 5:12–13). Reflecting upon them or their ways has more provocation than edification in it. A censorious humour is certainly most partial to itself, and self-indulgent; it can sooner endure a great beam in its own eye than a little mote in its neighbour's; and this shows evidently that it is not the hatred of sin, or the love of virtue, which is the single and simple principle of it; but self-love, shrouded under the veil of displeasure at sin, and delight in virtue.

I would think one great help to amend this would be to abate much from the superfluity and multitude of discourses upon others. In the multitude of words there wants not sin, and in the multitude of discourses upon other men there cannot miss the sin of rash judging. I find the saints and fearers of God commended for speaking often one *to* another, but not at all for speaking *of* one another. The subject of their discourse (*Mal.* 3:16) certainly was of another strain, how good it was to serve the Lord, etc., opposite to the evil communication of others there registered.

5. *Charity is no tale-bearer*; it goes not about as a slanderer to reveal a secret, though true (*Prov.* 20:19). It

is of a faithful spirit to conceal the matter (*Prov.* 11:13). Another man's good name is as a pledge laid down in our hand, which every man would faithfully restore, and take heed how he lose it or alienate it by backbiting. Some would have nothing to say if they had not others' faults and frailties to declaim upon; but it were better that such kept always silent, that either they had no ears to hear of them, or know them, or had no tongues to vent them. If they do not lie grossly in it, they think they do no wrong. But let them judge it in reference to themselves: 'A good name is better than precious ointment' (*Eccles.* 7:1), and 'rather to be chosen than great riches' (*Prov.* 22:1). And is that no wrong, to defile that precious ointment, and to rob or steal away that jewel more precious than great riches?

There is a strange connection between these: 'Thou shalt not go up and down as a talebearer, nor stand against the blood of thy neighbour' (*Lev.* 19:16). It is a kind of murder, because it kills that which is as precious as life to an ingenuous heart. 'The words of a talebearer are as wounds, and they go down to the innermost parts of the belly' (*Prov.* 18:8; 26:22). They strike a wound to any man's heart that can hardly be cured; and there is nothing that is such a seminary of contention and strife among brethren as this. It is the oil to feed the flame of alienation; take away a talebearer, and strife ceases (*Prov.* 26:20). Let there be but any (as there want not such who have no other trade or occupation) to whisper into the ears of brethren, and suggest evil apprehensions of them, they will separate chief friends, as we see it in daily experience (*Prov.* 16:28). Revilers are amongst those who are excluded out of the kingdom of God (*1 Cor.* 6:10). And therefore, as the Holy Ghost gives general precepts for the profitable and edifying improvement of the tongue, that so it may indeed be the glory of a man – which truly is no small point of religion, as James shows: 'If any man offend not in word, the same is a perfect man' (*James* 3:2) – so that same Spirit gives us particular directions about this, 'Speak not evil one of another, brethren. He that speaketh evil of his brother, and judgeth his brother, speaks evil of the law, and judges the law' (*James* 4:11); because he puts himself in the place of the Lawgiver, and his own judgment and fancy in the room of the law, and so judges the law. Therefore, the apostle Peter makes a wise and significant connection (*1 Pet.* 2:1): 'Laying aside all malice, and all guile, and hypocrisies, and envies, and all evil speakings . . .'

Truly, evil speaking of our brethren, though it may be true, yet it proceeds out of the abundance of these in the heart: guile, hypocrisy, and envy. While we catch at a name of piety from censuring others, and build our own reputation upon the ruins of another's good name, hypocrisy and envy are too predominant. If we would indeed grow in grace by the Word, and taste more how gracious the Lord is, we must lay these aside, and become as little children, without guile and without gall. Many account it excuse enough that they did not invent evil tales, or were not the first broachers of them; but the

Scripture joins both together, the man that shall abide in God's tabernacle must neither vent nor invent them, neither cast them down nor take them up: 'He backbiteth not with his tongue . . . nor taketh up a reproach against his neighbour' (*Psa.* 15:3); or *receives not*, or *endures not*, as in the margin; he neither gives it nor receives it; has not a tongue to speak of others' faults, nor an ear to hear them; indeed, he has a tongue to confess his own, and an ear open to hear another confess his faults, according to that precept, 'Confess your faults one to another.' We are forbidden to have much society or fellowship with tale-bearers; and it is added (*Prov.* 20:19), 'And meddle not with such as flatter with their mouth', as indeed commonly they who reproach the absent, flatter the present; a back-biter is a face-flatterer, and therefore, we should not only not meddle with such, but drive them away as enemies to human society.

Charity would in such a case protect itself, if I may so say, by an angry countenance, an appearance of anger and real dislike; as the north wind drives away rain, so that entertainment would drive away a backbiting tongue (*Prov.* 25:23). If we do discountenance it, backbiters will be discouraged to open their pack of news and reports; and, indeed, the receiving readily of evil reports of brethren is a partaking of the unfruitful works of darkness, which we should rather reprove (*Eph.* 5:11). To join with the teller is to complete the evil report; for if there were no receiver, there would be no teller, no tale-bearer. 'Charity shall cover the multitude of sins' (*1 Pet.* 4: 8); and therefore, 'Above all things, have fervent charity among yourselves', says he. What is above prayer and watching unto the end, above sobriety? Indeed, in reference to fellowship with God, these are above all; but, in relation to comfortable fellowship one with another in this world, this is above all, and the crown or cream of other graces. He whose sins are covered by God's free love cannot think it hard to spread the garment of his love over his brother's sins. Hatred stirs up strife, and all uncharitable affections, as envy, wrath; it stirs up contentions, and blazes abroad men's infirmities. But love covers all sins, conceals them from all to whom the knowledge of them does not belong (*Prov.* 10:12). Love, in a manner, suffers not itself to know what it knows, or at least to remember it much; it will sometimes hoodwink itself to a favourable construction; it will pass by an infirmity, and refuse to recognize it, while many stand still and commune with it; but he that covers a transgression seeks love to bury offences in.

Silence is a notable mean to preserve concord, and beget true amity and friendship, The keeping of faults long above ground unburied doth make them cast forth such an evil savour as will ever part friends. Therefore, says the wise man, 'He that covereth a transgression seeketh love, but he that repeateth a matter separateth very friends' (*Prov.* 17:9). Covering faults Christianly will make a stranger a friend, but repeating and blazing of them, will make a friend not only a stranger but an enemy. Yet this is nothing to the prejudice of that Christian duty of reproving and admonishing one another (*Eph.* 5:11): 'Have no fellowship with the unfruitful works of darkness, but rather reprove them.' Love commands to reprove 'in the spirit of meekness' (*Gal.* 6:1), as a man would restore an arm out of joint. And, therefore, 'Thou shalt not hate thy brother in thine heart: thou shalt in any wise rebuke thy neighbour, and not suffer sin upon him' (*Lev.* 19:17). And he that reproves his brother after this manner from love, and in meekness and wisdom, shall afterward find more favour of him than he that flatters with his tongue (*Prov.* 28:23). To cover grudges and jealousies in our hearts is to nourish a flame in our bosom, which only waits for a vent, and will, at one occasion or other, burst out.

But to look too narrowly to every step, and to write up a register of men's mere frailties, especially so as to publish them to the world: that is inconsistent with the rule of love. And truly, it is a token of one destitute of wisdom to despise his neighbour; but a man of understanding will hold his peace. He that has most defects himself will find most in others, and strive to vilify them one way or other; but a wise man can pass by frailties, yea, offences done to him, and be silent (*Prov.* 11:12).

5

HUMILITY AND MEEKNESS

Humility is the root of charity, and meekness the fruit of both. There is no solid and pure ground of love to others unless the rubbish of self-love is first cast out of a soul; and when that 'superfluity of naughtiness' is cast out, then charity has a solid and deep foundation. 'The end of the commandment is charity out of a pure heart' (*1 Tim.* 1:5). It is only such a purified heart, cleansed from that poison and contagion of pride and self-estimation, that can send out such a sweet and wholesome stream, to the refreshing of the spirits and bowels of the church of God.

If self-glory and pride have deep roots fastened into the soul, they draw all the sap and virtue downward, and send little or nothing up to the tree of charity, which makes it barren and unfruitful in the works of righteousness, and fruits of mercy and meekness. There are obstructions in the way of that communication which can only be removed by the plucking up of this root of pride and self-estimation, which preys upon all, and incorporates all in itself; and yet, like the lean kine that had devoured the fat, it is never the fatter or more well-favoured (*Gen.* 41:1–4).

1. *How Christ Teaches Humility*

It is no wonder then that these are the first principles that we must learn in Christ's school, the very A B C of Christianity: 'Learn of me; for I am meek and lowly in heart: and ye shall find rest unto your souls' (*Matt.* 11:29). This is the great Prophet sent of the Father into the world to teach us, whom he has, with a voice from heaven, commanded us to hear, 'This is my well-beloved Son, hear him.' Should not the fame and report of such a teacher move us?

He was testified of very honourably long before he came, that he had the Spirit above measure, that he had the tongue of the learned (*Isa.* 50:4); that he was a greater prophet than Moses (*Deut.* 18:15,18); that is, the Wonderful Counsellor of heaven and earth (*Isa.* 9:6); the witness to the people, a teacher and leader to the people. And then, when he came, he had the most glorious testimony from the most glorious Persons, the Father, and the Holy Ghost, in the most solemn manner that ever the world heard of (*Matt.* 17:5), 'Behold a voice out of the cloud, which said, This is my beloved Son, in whom I am well pleased; hear ye him.' Now, this is our Master, our Rabbi (*Matt.* 23:8).

This is 'the Apostle and High Priest of our profession' (*Heb.* 3:1). The 'light of the world' and life of men (*John* 8:12; 6:33,51). Having then such a Teacher and Master, sent us from heaven, may we not glory in our Master? But some may suppose that he who came down from heaven, filled with all the riches and treasures of heavenly wisdom, would reveal in his school to his disciples, all the mysteries and profound secrets of nature and art, about which the world has plodded since the first taste of the tree of knowledge, and beaten out their brains, to the vexation of all their spirits, without any fruit but the discovery of the impossibility of knowing, and the increase of sorrow by searching.

Who would not expect, when the Wisdom of God descends among men, but that he should show to the world that wisdom in the understanding of all the works of God which all men have been pursuing in vain; that he by whom all things were created, and so could unbowel and manifest all their hidden causes and virtues, all their admirable and wonderful qualities and operations, as easily by a word as he made them by a word: who would not expect, I say, but that he should have made this world, and the mysteries of it, the subject of all his lessons, the more to illustrate his own glorious power and wisdom?

And yet, behold, they who had come into his school and heard this Master and Doctor teach his scholars, they who had been invited to come, through the fame and report of his name, would have stood astonished and surprised to hear the subject of his doctrine; one come from on high to teach such low things as these: 'Learn of me, I am meek and lowly.' Other men that are masters of professions, and authors of sects or orders, do aspire to some singularity in doctrine to make them famous. But, behold our Lord and Master, this is the doctrine he vents. It has nothing in it that sounds high and looks big in the estimation of the world. In regard to the wisdom of the world, it is foolishness. A doctrine of humility from the Most High! A lesson in lowliness and meekness from the Lord and Maker of all! There seems, at first, nothing in it to allure any to follow it. Who would travel so far as the college of Christianity to learn no more than this, when every man pretends to be a teacher of it? But, truly, there is a majesty in this lowliness, and there is a singularity in this commonness. If ye would stay and hear a little longer, and enter into a deep search of this doctrine, ye would be surcharged and overcome with wonder. It seems shallow till you enter, but it has no bottom.

Christianity makes no great noise, but it runs the deeper. It is a light and superficial knowledge of it, a small smattering of the doctrine of it, that makes men despise it and prefer other things; but the deep and solid apprehension of it will make us adore and admire, and drive us to an *O altitudo!* 'O the depth of the riches both of the wisdom and knowledge of God' (*Rom.* 11:33)!

As the superficial knowledge of nature makes men atheists, but the profound understanding of it makes men pious, so all other things *vilescunt scientia*, grow more contemptible by the knowledge of them; it is ignorance of them which is the mother of that devout admiration we bear to them, but of Christianity only can it be said:

Vilescit ignorantia, clarescit scientia [1]

It is common and base, because not known; and that is no disparagement at all unto it, that there is none despises it but he that knows it not, and none can do any thing but despise all besides it, that once knows it; that is the proper excellency and glory of it.

All arts and sciences have their principles and common axioms of unquestionable authority. All kinds of professions have some fundamental doctrines and points which are the character of them. Christianity has its principles too, and principles must be plain and uncontroverted. They must be evident by their own light, and apt to give light to other things; all the rest of the conclusions of the art are but derivations and deductions from them. Our Master and Doctor follows the same method. He lays down some common principles, some fundamental points of this profession, upon which all the building of Christianity hangs: 'Learn of me, for I am meek and lowly.' This was the high lesson that his life preached so exemplarily and his doctrine pressed so earnestly; and in this he is very unlike other teachers who impose burdens on others, and themselves do not so much as touch them. But he first practises his doctrine, and then preaches it; he first

[1] It becomes contemptible through ignorance, but glorious through knowledge.

casts a pattern in himself, and then presses to follow it. Examples teach better than rules, but both together are most effectual and sure. The rarest example and noblest rule that ever were given to men are here met together.

2. *The Nature of Humility and of Pride*

The rule is about a thing that has a low name, but a high nature. Lowliness and meekness in reputation and outward form are like servants; yet they account it no robbery to be equal with the highest and most princely graces. The vein of gold and silver lies very low in the bowels of the earth, but it is not, therefore, base, but the more precious. Other virtues may come with more observation; but these, like the Master that teaches them, come with more reality; if they have less pomp, they have more power and virtue. Humility, how suitable it is to humanity! They are as near of kin one to another, as *homo* and *humus*;[1] and therefore, except a man cast off humanity, and forget his original – the ground – the dust from whence he was taken, I do not see how he can shake off humility. Self-knowledge is the mother of it. The knowledge of that *humus* [earth] would make us *humiles* [humble men]; look to the hole of the pit from whence you are hewn; a man could not look high that looked so low as the pit from whence we were taken by nature, even the dust; and the pit from whence we are hewn by grace,

[1] The Latin word *homo* (man) was thought to be derived from *humus* (the earth), because Adam was formed of 'the dust of the ground' (*Gen.* 2:7).

even man's lost and ruined state. Such a low look would make a lowly mind. Therefore pride must be nothing else but an empty and vain tumour, a puffing up. 'Knowledge puffeth up'; not self-knowledge: that casts down, and brings down all superstructures, razes out all vain confidence to the very foundation, and then begins to build on a solid ground. But knowledge of other things without, joined with ignorance of ourselves within, is but a swelling, not a growing; it is a bladder or skin full of wind. A blast or breath of an airy applause or commendation will extend it and fill it full. And what is this else but a monster in humanity; the skin of a man stuffed or blown up with wind and vanity, to the shadow and resemblance of a man, but no bones or sinews, nor real substance within?

Pride is an excrescence; it is nature swelled beyond the intrinsic terms or limits of magnitude, the spirit of a mouse in a mountain. Now, if any thing goes beyond the just bounds of the magnitude set to it, it is imperfect, disabled in its operations, vain and unprofitable, yea, a prodigy or a monster. If there is not so much real excellency as may fill up the circle of our self-estimation, then surely, it must be full of emptiness and vanity; fancy and imagination must supply the vacant room where solid worth cannot extend so far. Now, I believe, if any man could but impartially and seriously reflect upon himself, he would see nothing of that kind, no true solid and real dignity to provoke love; but real baseness and misery to procure loathing. There is a lie in every sin: but the greatest and grossest lie is committed in pride, and attributing that excellency to ourselves which is not. And upon what erroneous fancy, which is a sandy and vain foundation, is built the tower of self-estimation, vain glorying, and such like! Pride, which is the mother of these, says most presumptuously, 'By the strength of my hand I have done it, and by my wisdom; for I am prudent' (*Isa.* 10:13). 'I am, and none else besides me' (*Isa.* 47:10). It is such a false imagination, 'I am of perfect beauty', 'I am a God' (*Ezek.* 27:3; 28:2), which swells and lifts up the heart. Now, what a vain thing it is, an inordinate elevation of the heart upon a false misapprehension of the mind: 'His soul which is lifted up is not upright in him' (*Hab*: 2:4). It must be a tottering building that is founded on such a gross mistake.

3. *Pride's Pretension, and How It May Be Humbled*

Some cover their pride with the pretence of high spiritedness, and please themselves in the apprehension of some magnanimity and generosity. But the truth is, it is not true magnitude, but a swelling out of a superabundance of pestilent humours. True greatness of spirit is inwardly and throughout solid, firm from the bottom, and the foundation of it is truth. Which of the two, do you think, has the better spirit, he that calls dust, dust, and accounts of dung as dung; or he that, upon a false imagination, thinks dust and dung is gold and silver, esteems himself a rich man, and raises up himself above others?

Humility is the only true magnanimity; for it digs down low, that it may set and establish the foundation of true worth. It is true it is lowly, and bows down low; but as with water that comes from a height, the lower it comes down the higher it ascends up again; so, the humble spirit, the lower it falls in its own estimation, the higher it is raised in real worth and in God's estimation. 'Whosoever shall exalt himself shall be abased; and he that shall humble himself shall be exalted' (*Matt.* 23:12). He is like a growing tree: the deeper the roots go down in the earth, the higher the tree grows above ground; as Jacob's ladder, the foot of it is fastened in the earth, but the top of it reaches the heavens.

And this is the sure way to ascend to heaven. Pride would fly up upon its own wings; but the humble man will enter at the lowest step, and so goes up by degrees, and in the end it is made manifest. Pride catches a fall, and humility is raised on high; it descended that it might ascend. 'A man's pride shall bring him low: but honour shall uphold the humble in spirit' (*Prov.* 29:23). 'Pride goeth before destruction, and an haughty spirit before a fall'; but 'before honour is humility' (*Prov.* 16:18 and 18:12). The first week of creation, as it were, afforded two signal examples of this wise permutation of divine justice: angels cast out of heaven, and a man out of paradise. A high and wretched aim at wisdom brought both as low as hell; the pride of angels and men was but the rising up to a height, or climbing up a steep to the pinnacle of glory, that they might catch the lower fall. But the last week of the creation, so to speak, shall afford us rare and eminent demonstrations of the other: poor, wretched, and miserable sinners lifted up to heaven by humility, whereas angels were thrown down from heaven for pride. What a strange sight! An angel, once so glorious, so low; and a sinner, once so wretched and miserable, so high! Truly may a man conclude within himself, 'Better it is to be of an humble spirit with the lowly, than to divide the spoil with the proud' (*Prov.* 16:19). Happy lowliness, that is the foundation of true happiness; but miserable highness, that is the beginning of eternal baseness. 'Blessed are the poor in spirit: for theirs is the kingdom of heaven' (*Matt.* 5:3). Blessedness begins low in poverty of spirit: and Christ's sermon upon blessedness begins at it, but it arises in the end to the riches of a kingdom, a heavenly kingdom.

Grace is the seed of glory; and poverty of spirit is the seed, first dead, before it is quickened to grow up in the fruits. And, indeed, the grain 'is not quickened, except it die' (*1 Cor.* 15:36), and then it gets a body, and 'bringeth forth much fruit' (*John* 12:24). Even so, grace is sown into the heart, but it is not quickened except it die in humility, and then God gives it a body, when it springs up in other beautiful graces – of meekness, patience, love, etc. But these are never ripe till the day that the soul gets the warm beams of heaven, being separated from the body, and then is the harvest, a rich crop of blessedness.

Holiness is the ladder to go up to happiness by; or rather, our Lord Jesus Christ, as adorned with all these graces. Now, the steps of it are mentioned in Matthew 5; and the lowest step that a soul first ascends to him by is poverty of spirit, or humility. And truly, the spirit cannot meet with Jesus Christ till he first bring it down low, because he has come so low himself, so that no soul can ascend up to heaven by him unless they bow down to his lowliness, and rise upon that step.

Now, a man being thus humbled in spirit before God, and under his mighty hand, he alone is fit to obey the apostolic precept, 'All of you be subject one to another' (*1 Pet.* 5:5). Humility towards men depends upon that poverty and self-emptying under God's mighty hand (verse 6). It is only a lowly heart that can make the back to bow, and submit to others of whatsoever quality, and 'condescend to them of low estate' (*Rom.* 12:16; *Eph.* 5:21). But the fear of the Lord, humbling the spirit, will easily set it as low as any other can put it. This is the only basis and foundation of Christian submission and moderation. It is not a complimental condescension. It does not consist in an external show of gesture and voice; that is but an apish imitation. And, indeed, pride will often palliate itself under voluntary shows of humility, and can demean itself to uncomely and unseemly submissions to persons far inferior; but it is the more deformed and hateful that it lurks under some shadows of humility. As an ape is the more ugly and ill-favoured, in that it is more like a man, because it is not a man; so vices have more deformity in them when they put on the garb and vizard of virtue; only, it may appear how beautiful a garment true humility is, when pride desires often to be covered with the appearance of it, to hide its nakedness.

4. *The Excellence of True Humility*

Oh, how rich a clothing is the mean-seeming garment of humility and poverty of spirit! 'Be clothed with humility' (*1 Pet.* 5:5). It is the ornament of all graces; it covers a man's nakedness by uncovering it. If a man had all other endowments, this one dead fly would make all the ointment unsavoury, pride; but humility is *condimentum virtutum*, as well as *vestimentum*;[1] it seasons all graces, and covers all infirmities. Garments are both for ornament and necessity; truly this clothing is fit for both, to adorn and beautify whatever is excellent, and to hide or supply whatsoever is deficient, *ornamentum et perimentum.*[2]

The apostle Paul gives a solemn charge to the Romans, (*Rom.* 12:3), not to think too highly of themselves, but soberly. An extreme undervaluing and denial of all worth in ourselves, though it is suitable before God (*Luke* 17: 6–10; *Prov.* 30:2–3; *Job* 42:6; *1 Cor.* 3:7); yet it is uncomely and incongruous before men. Humility does not exclude all knowledge of any excellency in itself, or defect in another it can discern; but this is its worth, that it thinks soberly of the one, and despises not the other. The humble man knows any advantage he has beyond another, but he is not wise in his own conceit. He looks not so much on that side of things, his own perfections and others' imperfections. That is very dangerous. But he casts his eye most on the other side, his own infirmities and others' virtues, his worst part and their best part, and this makes

[1] The seasoning of the virtues, as well as their garment.
[2] An ornament and covering.

up an equality or proportion. Where there is inequality, there is a different measure of gifts and graces, there are diverse failings and infirmities, and degrees of them. Now, how shall such unequal members make up one body, and join in one harmonious being, unless this proportion is kept, that the defects of one are made up by the humility of another? The difference and inequality is taken away this way, by fixing my eye most upon my own disadvantages and my brother's advantages. If I be higher in any respect, yet certainly, I am lower in some, and therefore the unity of the body may be preserved by humility. I will consider in what I come short, and in what another excels, and so I can condescend to them of low degree. This is the substance of that which is subjoined (*Rom.* 12:16), 'Mind not high things, but condescend to men of low estate. Be not wise in your own conceits.' And this allows us in honour to prefer one another, taking ourselves up in the notion of what evil is in us, and another up in the notion of what good is in him. 'Be kindly affectioned one to another with brotherly love; in honour preferring one another' (*Rom.* 12:10). Thus there may be an equality of mutual respect and love, where there is an inequality of gifts and graces. There may be one measure of charity where there are different measures of faith, because both neglect that difference, and pitch upon their own evils and another's good.

It is our custom to 'compare ourselves among ourselves' and the result of that secret comparison is esteeming ourselves and despising others. We take our measure, not by our own real and intrinsic qualifications, but by the stature of other men's; and if we find any disadvantage in others, or any pre-eminency in ourselves, in such a partial application and comparison of ourselves with others (as self-love will readily, if it does not find it, fancy it), then we have a tacit glorying within ourselves, and a secret complacency in ourselves. But the humble Christian dares not make himself of that number, nor 'boast of things without his measure'; he dare not think himself good because *deterioribus melior*,[1] better than others who are worse. But he judges himself by that intrinsic measure which God has distributed to him, and so finds reason for sobriety and humility; and therefore he dare not stretch himself beyond his measure, or go without his station and degree (*2 Cor.* 10:12–14).

Humility makes a man compare himself with the best, that he may find how bad he himself is, but pride measures by the worst, that it may hide from a man his own imperfections. The one takes a perfect rule, and finds itself nothing; the other takes a crooked rule, and imagines itself something. But this is the way that unity may be kept in the body, if all the members keep this method and order, the lowest to measure by him that is higher, and the higher to judge himself by him that is yet above him; and he that is above all the rest to compare with the rule of perfection, and find himself further short of the rule than the lowest is below him. If our comparisons did thus ascend, we would descend in humility, and all the differ-

[1] Better than the worse.

ent degrees of persons would meet in one centre of low-liness of mind. But while our rule descends, our pride ascends. The Scripture holds out pride and self-estimation as the root of many evils, and humility as the root of many good fruits among men. Only through pride comes contention (*Prov.* 13:10). There is pride at least in one of the parties, and often in both; it makes one man careless of another and, out of contempt, not to study equity and righteousness towards him; and it makes another man impatient of receiving and bearing an injury or disrespect. While every man seeks to please himself, the contention arises. Pride in both parties makes both stiff and inflexible to peace and equity; and in this there is a great deal of folly; for by this means, both procure more real displeas-ure and dissatisfaction to their own spirits. But 'with the well-advised is wisdom'. They who have discretion and judgment will not be so wedded to their own conceits but that in humility they can forbear and forgive for the sake of peace. And though this seem harsh and bitter at first, to a passionate and distempered mind, yet, oh, how sweet it is after! There is a greater sweetness and refreshment in the peaceable condescension of a man's spirit and the quiet passing by of an injury than the highest satisfaction that ever revenge or contention gave to any man. 'When pride cometh, then cometh shame: but with the lowly is wisdom' (*Prov.* 11:2).

When pride grows to maturity and ripeness, shame is near at hand, almost as near as the harvest; if pride comes up, shame is in the next rank behind it. But there is a great wisdom in lowliness. That is the honourable society that it walks in. There may be a secret connection between this and the former verse, 'A false balance is abomination to the LORD: but a just weight is his delight.' Now, if it be so in such low things as merchandise, how much more abominable is a false spiritual balance in the weighing of ourselves? Pride has a false balance in its hand: the weight of self-love carries down the one scale by a long way.

Lowliness of mind is the strongest bond of peace and charity; it banishes away strife and vain-glory, and makes each man to esteem another better than himself (*Phil.* 2: 3), because the humble man knows his own inside, and only another's outside. Now, certainly the outside is always better and more specious than the inside; and therefore a humble man, seeing nothing but his neighbour's outside, and being acquainted thoroughly with his own inside, he esteems another better than himself. Humility, as it makes a man think well of another, so it hinders him from speaking evil of his brother (*James* 4:10). James lays down the ground-work in the tenth verse, 'Humble yourselves in the sight of the Lord, and he shall lift you up.' He raises his superstructure in verses 11 and 12, 'Speak not evil one of another, brethren. He that speaketh evil of his brother, and judgeth his brother, speaketh evil of the law, and judgeth the law: but if thou judge the law, thou art not a doer of the law, but a judge. There is one law-giver, who is able to save, and to destroy: who art thou that judgest another?' For truly the very ground of evil-speaking of that kind is some advantage we think may redound to our own reputation by the diminution of another's fame; or, because we are so short-sighted in ourselves, therefore we are sharp-sighted towards others; and because we think little of our own faults, we are ready to aggravate other men's to an extremity. But, in so doing, we take the place of the judge and law upon us, which judges others and is judged by none. So we judge others, and not ourselves, neither will we suffer ourselves to be judged by others. This is to make ourselves the infallible rule, to judge the law.

Humility levels men to a holy subjection and submission to one another, without any confusion of their different degrees and stations. It teaches men to give that respect and regard to every one that is due to his place or worth; and to signify it in such a way as may testify the simplicity of their estimation and the sincerity of their respect (*Eph.* 5:21): 'Submit yourselves one to another in the fear of God.' *1 Pet.* 5:5: 'All of you be subject one to another, and be clothed with humility.' Now, if humility can put a man below others, certainly it will make him endure patiently and willingly to be placed in that same rank by others. When others give him that place to sit in that he had chosen for himself, will he conceive himself wronged and affronted, though others about him think so? Nay, it is hard to persuade him of an injury of that kind, because the apprehension of such an affront has for its foundation the imagination of some excellency beyond others, which lowliness has razed out. He has placed himself so low for every man's edification and instruction that others can put him no lower; and there he sits quietly and peaceably. *Bene qui latuit, bene vixit.*[1] Affronts and injuries fly over him, and light upon the taller cedars, while the shrubs are safe. *Qui cadit in plano (vix hoc tamen evenit ipsum), sic cadit, ut tacta surgere possit humo.*[2] He sits so low that he cannot fall lower; so a humble man's fall upon the ground is no fall indeed, except in the apprehension of others; but it is a heavy and bruising fall from off the tower of self-conceit.

Now the example that is given us, 'Learn of me', is certainly of greater force to persuade a man to this humble, composed, and quiet temper of spirit, than all the rules in the world: that the Son of God should come down and act it before our eyes, and cast us a pattern of humility and meekness. If this does not prevail to humble the heart, I know not what can. Indeed, this root of bitterness, which is in all men's hearts by nature, is very hard to pluck up; yea, when other weeds of corruption are extirpated, this poisonous one, pride, grows the faster, and roots the deeper. Suppose a man should be stripped naked of all the garments of the old man, this would be certainly nearest his skin, and last to put off. It is so pestilent an evil that it grows in the glass window as well as on the dunghill; and, which is strange, it can spring out of the heart, and take moisture and aliment from humility as well as from other

---

[1] He who has lived out of sight has lived well. [2] He who falls on a flat place (though this rarely happens) can rise again from the ground he has landed on. (Both of these are quotations from Ovid.)

graces. A man is in danger of being proud that he is not proud, and being high-minded because he is lowly; therefore it is not good to reflect much on our own graces, any more than for a man to eat much honey.

I know no antidote so sovereign as the example of Jesus Christ to cure this evil; and he himself often proposes this recipe to his disciples (*John* 13:13–17): 'Ye call me Master and Lord: and ye say well; for so I am. If I then, your Lord and Master, have washed your feet, ye also ought to wash one another's feet. For I have given you an example, that ye should do as I have done to you. Verily, verily, I say unto you, the servant is not greater than his lord; neither he that is sent greater than he that sent him. If ye know these things, happy are ye if ye do them.' *Matt.* 11:29–30: 'Take my yoke upon you, and learn of me, for I am meek and lowly in heart: and ye shall find rest unto your souls. For my yoke is easy, and my burden is light.' *Matt.* 20:27–28: 'And whosoever will be chief among you, let him be your servant: even as the Son of man came not to be ministered unto, but to minister, and to give his life a ransom for many.' I wish that might always sound in our ears: 'The servant is not above his lord'; 'The Son of man came not to be ministered unto but to minister.'

Oh, whose spirit would not that compose? What apprehension of wrong would it not compensate? What flame of contention about worth and respect would it not quench? What noise of tumultuous passions would it not silence? Therefore, the apostle of the Gentiles prescribes this medicine (*Phil.* 2:5–8): 'Let this mind be in you, which was also in Christ Jesus: who, being in the form of God, thought it not robbery to be equal with God: but made himself of no reputation, and took upon him the form of a servant, and was made in the likeness of men; and being found in fashion as a man, he humbled himself, and became obedient unto death, even the death of the cross.' If he did humble himself out of charity, who was so high, how should we humble ourselves, both out of charity and necessity, who are so low! If we knew ourselves, it would not be strange that we were humble. The evidence of truth would extort it from us. But here is the wonder, that he who knew himself to be equal to God, should notwithstanding become lower than men; that the Lord of all should become the servant of all, and the King of Glory make himself of no reputation; that he pleased to come down lowest who knew himself to be the highest of all. No necessity could persuade it, but charity and love has done it. Now, then, how monstrous and ugly a thing must pride be after this! That the dust should raise itself, and a worm swell; that wretched, miserable man should be proud when it pleased the glorious God to be humble; that absolute necessity did not constrain to this; that simple love persuaded him! How this heightens and elevates humility, that such a One gives out himself, not only as the Teacher, but as the Pattern of it:

'LEARN OF ME, FOR I AM MEEK AND LOWLY
IN HEART, AND YE SHALL FIND REST
UNTO YOUR SOULS.'

THE SINNER'S SANCTUARY

SERMON 37

For as many as are led by the Spirit of God, they are the sons of God. For ye have not received the spirit of bondage again to fear; but ye have received the Spirit of adoption, whereby we cry, Abba, Father (Rom. 8:14–15).

The life of Christianity, taken in itself, is the most pleasant and joyful life that can be, exempted from those fears and cares, those sorrows and anxieties, that all other lives are subject to; for this is necessarily the force and efficacy of true religion, if it be true to its name, to disburden and ease the heart, and give all manner of consolation. Certainly it is most completely furnished with all the variety of delights to entertain a soul that can be imagined.

¹ This exposition and the two which follow are Sermons 37, 39 and 40 from *The Sinner's Sanctuary*, a series of forty sermons on Romans 8:1–15, first published in 1670.

Yet I must confess that, while we consult with the experience and practice of Christians, this bold assertion seems to be much weakened, and too much ground is given to confirm the contrary misapprehensions of the world, who take it to be a sullen, melancholic, and disconsolate life, attended with many fears and sorrows.

It is, alas! too evident that many Christians are kept in bondage, almost all their lifetime, through fear of eternal death. How many dismal representations of sin and wrath are in the souls of some Christians, which keep them in much thraldom! At least, who is it that is not once and often brought into bondage after conversion, and made to apprehend fearfully their own estate? Who has such constant, uninterrupted peace and joy in the Holy Ghost, or lies under such direct beams of divine favour, that these are not sometimes eclipsed, and their souls filled with the darkness of horror and terror? And truly the most part taste not so much sweetness in religion as makes them incessant and unwearied in the ways of godliness.

Yet notwithstanding of all this, we must vindicate Christianity itself, and not impute these things to it which are the infirmities and faults of its followers, who do not make the use of it that they should, and of which it is in itself capable.

Indeed, it is true that often we are brought to fear again, yet it is also certain that our allowance is larger, and that we have received the Spirit, not to put us in bondage again to fear, but rather to seal to our hearts that love of God which may not only expel fear, but bring in joy. I wish that this were deeply considered by all of us, that there is such a life as this attainable; that the Word of God does not deceive us in promising fair things which it cannot perform, but that there is a certain reality in the life of Christianity, in that peace and joy, tranquillity and serenity of mind that is held out to us, and that some have really found it and do find it; and that the reason why all of us do not find it in experience is not because it does not exist but because we have so little apprehension of it and diligence after it.

It is strange that all men who have pursued satisfaction in the things of this life, being disappointed, and one generation witnessing this to another, and one person to another, that notwithstanding men are this day as fresh in the pursuit of that, as big in their expectations, as ever. And yet in this business of religion, and the happiness to be found in it, though the oracles of God in all ages have testified from heaven how certain and possible it is, though many have found it in experience and left this on record to others, yet there is so slender a belief of the reality and certainty of it, and so slack a pursuit of it, as if we did not believe it at all.

Truly, my beloved, there is a great mistake in this, and it is general too. All men apprehend other things more feasible and attainable than personal holiness and happiness in religion; but truly, I conceive there is nothing in the world so practicable as this, nothing made so easy, so certain to a soul that really attends to it.

Let us take it so then. The fault is not religion's that those who profess it are subject to so much fear and care, and disquieted with so much sorrow; it is rather because Christianity does not sink into the hearts and souls of men, but only puts a tincture on their outside, or because the faith of divine truths is so superficial, and the consideration of them so slight, that they cannot have much efficacy and influence on the heart to quiet and compose it.

Is it any wonder that some souls are subject again to the bondage of fear and terror when they do not stand in awe to sin? Much liberty to sin will certainly embondage the spirit of a Christian to fear. Suppose a believer in Jesus Christ be exempted from the hazard of condemnation; yet he is the greatest fool in the world that would on that account venture on satisfaction to his lusts. For though it is true that he is not in danger of *eternal* wrath, yet he may find so much *present* wrath in his conscience as may make him think it was a foolish bargain. He may lose so much of the sweetness of the peace and joy of God as all the pleasures of sin cannot compensate.

Therefore to the end that you whose souls are once pacified by the blood of Christ, and composed by his word of promise, may so enjoy that constant rest and tranquillity as not to be enthralled again to your old fears and terrors, I would advise and recommend to you these two things:

1. *That ye would be much in the study of that allowance which the promises of Christ afford.* Be much in the

serious apprehension of the gospel, and certainly your doubts and fears would vanish at one stroke of such a rooted and established meditation. Think what you are called to, not to fear again, but to love rather, and honour him as a Father.

2. *And then, take heed to walk suitably, and preserve your seal of adoption unblotted, unrusted.* You should study so to walk as you may not cast dirt upon it, or open any gap in the conscience for the re-entry of those hellish-like fears and dreadful apprehensions of God. Certainly it is impossible to preserve the Spirit in freedom, if a man be not watchful against sin and corruption. David prays, 'Restore unto me the joy of thy salvation; and uphold me with thy free Spirit' (*Psa.* 51:12), as if his spirit had been abased, embondaged, and enthralled by the power of that corruption. If you would have your spirits kept free from the fear of wrath, study to keep them free from the power of sin, for that is but a fruit of this: and it is most suitable that the soul that cares not about being in bondage to sinful lusts should, by the righteousness of God, tempered with love and wisdom, be brought under the bondage he would not, that is, of fear and terror; for by this means the Lord makes him know how evil the first is, by the bitterness of the second.

It is usual, on such a Scripture as this, to propound many questions, and debate many practical cases; as, whether a soul, after believing, can be under legal bondage? And wherein these differ, the bondage of a soul after believing, and in its first conversion? And how far that bondage of fear is preparatory to faith? And many such questions. But I choose rather to hold forth the simple and naked truth for your edification, than put you upon or entertain you in such needless janglings and contentions.

All I desire to say to a soul in bondage is to exhort him to come to the Redeemer, and to consider that his case calls and cries for a delivery. Let him come, I say, and he shall find rest and liberty to his soul.

All I would say to souls delivered from this bondage is to request and beseech them to live in a holy fear of sins and jealousy over themselves, that so they may not be readily brought under the bondage of the fear of wrath again. Perfect love casts out the fear of hell, but perfect love brings in the fear of sin: 'Ye that love the LORD, hate evil' (*Psa.* 97:10); and if you hate it, you will fear it, in this state of infirmity and weakness wherein we are.

And if at any time you, through negligence and carelessness of walking, lose the comfortable evidence of the Father's love, and are reduced again to your old prison of legal terror, do not despair for that. Do not think that such a thing could not befall a child of God, and from that ground, do not raze former foundations; for the Scripture says not that whosoever believes once in Christ, and receives the Spirit of adoption, cannot fear again. We see it otherwise in David, in Heman, in Job, etc., all holy saints.

But the Scripture says, 'Ye have not received the spirit of bondage for that end', to fear again. It is not the allowance of your Father. Your allowance is better and larger, if you knew it, and did not sit below it.

Now, the great gift and large allowance of our Father is expressed in the next words, 'But ye have received the Spirit of adoption', etc. This Spirit of adoption is a Spirit of intercession, to make us cry to God as our Father. These are two gifts, adoption, or the privilege of sons, and the Spirit of adoption, revealing the love and mercy of God to the heart, and framing it to a son-like disposition.

Compare the two states together and it is a marvellous change: a rebel condemned, and then pardoned, and then adopted to be a son of God; a sinner under bondage, a bond-slave to sin and Satan, not only freed from that intolerable bondage, but advanced to this liberty, to be a son of God! This will be the continued wonder of eternity, and that whereabout the song of angels and saints will be. Accursed rebels, expecting nothing but present death, sinners arraigned and sentenced before his tribunal, and already tasting hell in their consciences and in fear of eternal perishing, not only to be delivered from that, but to be dignified with this privilege, to be the sons of God! To be taken from the gibbet to be crowned, that is the great mystery of wisdom and grace revealed in the gospel, the proclaiming whereof will be the joint labour of all the innumerable companies above for all eternity.

Now, if you ask how this estate is attainable, he himself tells us, John1:12, 'As, many as believed, or received, to them he gave the privilege to be the sons of God.' The way is made plain and easy; Christ the Son of God, the natural and eternal Son of God, became the son of man. To facilitate this, he hath taken on the burden of man's sin, the chastisement of our peace; and so, though the glorious Son of God, he became like the wretched and accursed sons of men; and therefore God hath proclaimed in the gospel, not only an immunity and freedom from wrath to all that, in the sense of their own misery, cordially receive him as he is offered; but the unspeakable privilege of sonship and adoption for his sake who became our elder brother (*Gal.* 4:4–5).

Men that lack children often supply their want by adopting some beloved friend in the place of a son; and this is a kind of supply of nature for the comfort of those who lack. But it is strange that God, having a Son so glorious, the very expression of his Person, and brightness of his glory, in whom he delighted from eternity; strange, I say, that he should in a manner lose and give away his only-begotten Son, that he might by this means adopt others, poor, despicable creatures, to be his sons and daughters. Certainly, this is an act infinitely transcending nature, such an act as has an unsearchable mystery in it, into which angels desire to look, and never cease looking, because they never see the bottom of it. It was not out of need he did it, not for any need he had of us, or comfort expected from us, but absolutely for our necessity and consolation, that he might have those upon whom to pour the riches of his grace.

THE SINNER'S SANCTUARY

SERMON 39

Whereby we cry, Abba, Father
(Rom. 8:15).

As there is a height of grace in bestowing such incomparably high dignities and excellent gifts on poor sinners as to make them the sons of God who were the children of the devil, and heirs of a kingdom who were heirs of wrath, so there is depth of wisdom in the Lord's allowance and manner of dispensing his love and grace in this life. For though the love is wonderful, that we should be called the sons of God, yet, as that apostle says, it does not yet so clearly appear what we shall be, by what we are (*1 John* 3:1). Our present condition is so unlike such a state and dignity, and our enjoyments so unsuitable to our rights and privileges, that it would not appear by the mean, low, and indigent state we are now in that we have so great and glorious a Father.

How many infirmities are we compassed about with! How many wants are we pressed with! Our necessities are infinite, and our enjoyments in no way proportioned to our necessities. Notwithstanding even this, the love and wisdom of our heavenly Father shows itself, and often-times more gloriously in the theatre of men's weakness, infirmities and wants, than they could appear in the abso-lute and total exemption of his children from necessities. Strength perfected in weakness, grace sufficient in infirmi-ties, has some greater glory than strength and grace alone. Therefore he hath chosen this way as most fit for the ad-vancing of his glory, and most suitable for our comfort and edification, to give us but little in hand, and environ us with a crowd of continued necessities and wants within and without, that we may learn to cry to him as our Father, and seek our supplies from him.

Besides, he has not been sparing but liberal in promises of hearing our cries, and supplying our wants. And so this way of narrow and hard dispensations, that at first seems contrary to the love and bounty and riches of our Father, in the perfect view of it appears to be the only way to per-petuate our communion with him, and often to renew the sense of his love and grace that would grow slack in our hearts if our needs did not every day stir up fresh longing. By this means also his answers to our prayers are so much the more refreshing.

There is a time of children's minority, when they stand in need of continual supplies from their parents or tutors, because they are not entered into possession of their inheritance. While they are in this state, there is nothing more fitting for them than in all their wants to address their father, and represent their wants to him. And it is fit they should live 'from hand to mouth', as we say, that they may know and acknowledge their dependence, on their father.

Truly, this is our minority, that is, our presence in the body, which, because of sin that dwells in it and its own natural weakness and incapacity, keeps us at such distance from the Lord that we cannot be intimately present with him. Now, in this condition, the comely and becoming exercise of children is to cry to our Father, to present all our grievances; and thus to enter into some holy correspondence with our absent Father, by the messenger of prayer and supplication, which cannot return empty, if it be not sent away too full of self-conceit.

This is the most natural breathing of a child of God in this world. It is the most proper acting of his new life, and the most suitable breathing out of that Spirit of adoption that is inspired into him, since there is so much life as to know what we want – and our wants are infinite. Therefore that life cannot but beat this way, in holy desires after God whose fullness can supply all wants.

This is the pulse of a Christian that beats continually, and there is much advantage to the continuity and uninterruptedness of the motion from the infiniteness and inexhaustedness of our needs in this life and the continual assaults that are made by necessity and temptation on the heart.

'But *ye* have received the Spirit of adoption, whereby *we* cry,' etc. He puts in his own name in the latter part, though theirs was in the former part. When he speaks of a donation or privilege, he applies it to the meanest, to show that the lowest and most despised creature is not in any incapacity to receive the greatest gifts of God. And then, when he mentions the working of that Spirit in the way of intercession, because it imports necessity and want, he cares not to commit some incongruity in the language, by changing the person ('ye' to 'we'), that he may teach us that weakness, infirmities and wants are common to the best and chiefest among Christians; that the most eminent have continual need to cry, and the lowest and most obscure believers have as good ground to believe in the hearing and acceptance of their cries as the greatest. The highest are not above the weakest and lowest ordinance, and the lowest are not below the comfort of help and acceptation in him.

Nay, the growth and increase of grace is so far from exempting men from, or setting them above, this duty of constant supplication that, on the contrary, this is just the measure of their growth and attainment in grace. As the degrees of the height of the River Nile in its overflowing are a sure sign of the fertility or barrenness of that year, so the overflowings of the Spirit of prayer in one gives a present account how the heart is, whether barren and unfruitful in the knowledge of Jesus Christ, or fruitful and lively and vigorous in it.

It is certain that contraries do discover one another, and

the more the one is increased, the more incompatible and inconsistent with the other it is seen to be, and the more perfect the discerning of it is. When grace is but as twilight in the soul, and as the dawning of the day only, gross darkness and uncleanness is seen; but the more it grows to the perfect day, the more sin is seen, and the more its hated ways are discovered that did not appear before. And therefore grace exercises itself the more in opposition to sin and in supplication to God.

To speak the truth, our growth here is but an advancement in the knowledge and sense of our poverty. It is but a further entry into the idolatrous temple of the heart, which makes a man see daily new abominations worse than the former; and therefore you may easily know that such repeated sights and discoveries will but press out more earnest and frequent cries from the heart, and such a growth in humility and faith in God's fullness will be but as oil to the flame of supplication. For what is prayer indeed, but the ardour of the affections after God, flaming up to him in cries and requests?

To speak of this exercise of a holy heart would require more of the spirit of it than we have. But truly this is to be lamented, that though there be nothing more common among Christians in the outward practice of it, yet that there is nothing more extraordinary and rare, even among many that use it, than to be acquainted with the inward nature of it. Truly, the most ordinary things in religion, are the greatest mysteries, as to the true life of them. We are strangers to the soul and life of those things which consist in the holy behaviour and deportment of our spirits before the Father of spirits.

The words of our text give some ground to speak of some special qualifications of prayer, and the chief principle of it:

The chief principle and original of prayer is the Spirit of adoption received into the heart.

It is a business of a higher nature than can be taught by precepts, or learned by custom and education. There is a general mistake among men, that the gift of prayer is attained by learning, and that it consists in the freedom and plenty of expression. But oh! how many doctors and disputers of the world that can defend all the articles of faith against the opposers of them, how unacquainted they are with this exercise, that the poor and unlearned, and nothings in the world, who cannot dispute for religion, yet they send up a more savoury and acceptable sacrifice, and sweet incense to God daily, when they offer up their soul's desires in simplicity and sincerity!

Certainly this is a spiritual thing, derived only from the Fountain of spirits. This grace of pouring out our souls unto him, and keeping communication with him, the variety of words and riches of expressions are but the shell of it, the external shadow; and all the life consists in the frame of the heart before God: and this none can put in frame but he that formed the spirit of man within him.

Some, through custom of hearing and using it, attain to a habit of expressing themselves readily in it, it may be, to the satisfaction of others, but, alas! they may be strangers to the first letters and elements of the life and spirit of prayer. I would have you who want both look up to heaven for it. Many of you cannot be induced to pray in your family (and I fear little or none in secret, which is indeed a more serious work) because you have not been used, or not learned, or such like. Alas, beloved, this comes not through education or learning. It comes from the Spirit of adoption, and if you cannot pray, you are saying you have not the Spirit, and if you have not the Spirit, you are not the sons of God. Know that *that* is the inevitable sequel of your own confession.

But I haste to the qualifications of this divine work, *fervency, reverence*, and *confidence*, in crying 'Abba, Father'; for these suit well towards our Father.

FERVENCY

The first, *fervency*, I fear, we must seek elsewhere than in prayer. I find it spent on other things of less moment. Truly, all the spirit and affection of men runs in another channel, in the ways of contention and strife, in the way of passion and miscalled zeal; and because these things whereabout we do thus earnestly contend have some interest or coherence with religion, we not only excuse but approve our vehemency. But, oh! much better if it were employed in supplications to God. That would be a divine channel!

Again, the marrow of other men's spirits is exhausted in the pursuit of things in the world. The edge of their desires is turned that way, and it must needs be blunted and dulled in spiritual things so that it cannot pierce into heaven and prevail effectually. I am sure this is the reason many of us are so cold in prayer. We do not warm ourselves, and how shall we think to prevail with God? Our spirits make little noise when we cry the loudest. We can scarce hear any whisper in our hearts, and how shall he hear us?

Certainly, it is not the extension of the voice that pleases him. It is the cry of the heart that is sweet harmony in his ears. And you may easily perceive that if you but consider that he is an infinite Spirit who pierces into all the corners of our hearts, and has all the darkness of it as light before him. How can you think that such a Spirit can be pleased with lip-cries? How can he endure such deceit and falsehood (who hath so perfect a contrariety with all false appearances), that your heart should lie so dead and flat before him, and the affection of it turned quite another way? There were no sacrifices without fire in the Old Testament, and that fire was kept alight perpetually; and so there should be no prayer now without some inward fire conceived in the desires, and blazing up and growing into a flame in the presenting of them to God.

The incense that was to be offered on the altar of perfume in Exodus 30 was to be *beaten and prepared*. And truly, prayer would do well to be made out of a beaten and bruised heart, and contrite spirit, a spirit truly sensible of its own unworthiness and wants; and that beating and pounding of the heart will yield a good, fragrant smell, as some spices only do when beaten.

The incense was made of *various spices*, intimating to us that true prayer is not one grace alone, but a compound of graces. It is the joint exercise of all a Christian's graces, seasoned with all. Every one of them gives some particular fragrancy to it, such as humility, faith, repentance, love, etc. The acting of the heart in supplication is a kind of compound and result of all these, as one perfume made up of many elements.

But above all, like the incense, our prayers must be *kindled by fire* on the altar; there must be some heat and fervour, some warmness conceived by the Holy Spirit in our hearts, which may make our spices send forth a pleasant smell, as many spices do only when they get heat.

Let us lay this engagement on our hearts, to be more serious in our addresses to God, the Father of spirits; above all, to present our inward soul before him, before whom it is naked and open, even if we do not bring it. And certainly *frequency* in prayer will much help us to fervency, and to keep it when we have it.

THE SINNER'S SANCTUARY

SERMON 40

Whereby we cry, Abba, Father
(Rom. 8:15).

All that know anything of religion must needs know and confess that there is no exercise either more suitable to him that professes it, or more needful for him, than to give himself to the exercise of *prayer*. But that which is confessed by all and, as to the outward performance, gone about by many, I fear is yet a mystery sealed up from us, as to the true and living nature of it.

There is much of it expressed here in few words, 'Whereby we cry, Abba, Father'. The divine constitution and qualifications of this divine work is here made up of a temper of *fervency, reverence* and *confidence*. The first I spoke of before; but I fear our hearts were not well heated then, or may be cooled since. It is not the loud noise of words that is best heard in heaven, or that is regarded as crying to God. No, this is transacted in the heart, more silently to men's ears, but it strikes up into the ears of God. His ear is sharp, and the voice of the soul's desires shrill, and though it were out of the depths, they will meet together. It is true, the vehemency of affection will sometimes cause the extension of the voice; but yet it may cry as loud to heaven when it is kept within.

I do not press such extraordinary degrees of fervour as may affect the body. I would rather that we accustomed ourselves to a solid, calm seriousness and earnestness of spirit, which might be more constant than such raptures can be, and that we might always gather our spirits to what we are about, and call them away from impertinent wanderings, and fix them upon the present object of our worship. This is to worship him in spirit, who is a Spirit.

REVERENCE

The other thing that composes the sweet temper of prayer is *reverence*. And what is more suitable, whether you consider him or yourselves? 'If then I be a father, where is mine honour? and if I be a master, where is my fear?' (*Mal.* 1:6). While we call him Father, or Lord, we proclaim this much, that we ought to know our distance from him, and his superiority to us. And if worship in prayer does not carry this character, and express this honourable and glorious Lord whom we serve, it lacks that congruity and suitableness to him that is the beauty of it. Is there anything more uncomely than for children to behave themselves irreverently and disrespectfully towards their fathers, to whom they owe themselves? It is a monstrous thing even in nature, and to nature's light. Oh, how much more abominable must it be to draw near to 'the Father of spirits', who made us, and not we ourselves, in whose hand our breath is, and whose are all our ways; in a word, to whom we owe not only this dust, but the living spirit that animates it, that was breathed from heaven, and finally, 'in whom we live, and move, and have our being', and well-being, to worship such a one, and yet to behave ourselves so unseemly and irreverently in the apprehension of his glory, by lying flat and dead before him, scarcely having him in our thoughts, to whom we speak them! And finally, our deportment in his sight is such as could not be admitted in the presence of any person a little above ourselves: to be about to speak to them, and yet to turn aside continually to every one that comes by, and entertain communication with every base creature; this, I say, in the presence of a king, or nobleman, would be accounted as absurd an incivility as could be committed; and yet we behave ourselves just so with the Father of spirits.

Oh, the wanderings of the hearts of men in divine worship, while we are in communication with our Father and Lord in prayer! Whose heart is fixed to a constant attendance and presence by the impression of his glorious holiness? Whose spirit does not continually gad abroad, and take note of every thing that occurs, and so mars that soul correspondence? Oh that this word were written with great letters on our hearts, 'God is greatly to be feared in the assembly of the saints, and to be had in reverence of all them that are about him' (*Psa.* 89:7)!

That one word, GOD, speaks all. Either we must convert him into an idol, which is nothing, or, if we apprehend him to be God, we must apprehend our infinite distance from him, and his unspeakable, inaccessible glory above us. He is greatly feared and reverenced in the assemblies that are above, in the upper courts of angels, those glorious spirits who must cover their feet from us, because we cannot see their glory. They must cover their faces from him, because they cannot behold his glory (*Isa.* 6). What a glorious train he has; and yet how reverent they are! They wait round about the throne, above and about it, as courtiers upon their king, for they are all ministering spirits, and they rest not day and night to adore and admire that holy One, crying, 'Holy, holy, holy, the whole earth is full of his glory.'

Now, how much more, then, should he be greatly feared and had in reverence in the assembly of his saints, of poor mortal men, whose foundation is in the dust and in the clay; and, besides, drink in iniquity like water! There are two points of difference and distance from us. He is nearer angels, for angels are pure spirits; but we have flesh, which is furthest removed from his nature. And then angels are holy and clean; yet that is but spotted to his unspotted holiness. But we are defiled with sin, which puts us furthest off from him, and which his holiness has greatest antipathy to. Let us consider this, my beloved, that we may carry the impression of the glorious holiness and majesty of God on our hearts whenever we appear before him, that so we may serve and 'rejoice with trembling', and pray with 'reverence and godly fear'. If we apprehend indeed our own quality and condition, how low, how base it is, how we cannot endure the very clear aspect of our own consciences, we cannot look on ourselves stedfastly without shame and confusion of face, at the deformed spectacle we behold; much less would we endure to have our souls opened and presented to the view of other men, even the basest of men. We would be overwhelmed with shame if they could see into our hearts! Now then, apprehend seriously what he is. How glorious in holiness! How infinite in wisdom! How the secrets of your souls are plain and open in his sight! And, I am persuaded, you will be composed to a reverent, humble, and trembling behaviour in his sight.

CONFIDENCE

But also, I must add this, that, because he is your Father, you may intermingle *confidence*. Nay, you are commanded so to do, and this honours him as much as reverence; for confidence in God as our Father is the best acknowledgment of the greatness and goodness of God. It declares how able he is to save us, and how willing, and so ratifies all the promises of God made to us, and sets a seal to his faithfulness.

There is nothing he accounts himself more honoured by than a soul's full resigning itself to him and relying upon his power and good-will in all necessities, casting its care upon him, as a loving Father who cares for us. And truly, there is much beauty and harmony in the juncture of these two, *rejoicing* with *trembling*, *confidence* with *reverence*, to ask 'nothing doubting', and yet sensible of our infinite distance from him and the disproportion of our requests to his highness.

A child-like disposition is composed thus, as also the temper and carriage of a courtier has these ingredients in it. The love of his Father, and the favour of his Prince, makes him take liberty, and assume boldness; and yet he is not unmindful of his own distance from his Father or Master. 'Let us draw near with . . . full assurance of faith' (*Heb.* 10:22). There is much in the Scripture – exhorted, commanded and commended – of that πληροφορια [plerophoria], that liberty and boldness of pouring out our requests to God, as one that certainly will hear us and grant that which is good.

Unbelief spoils all. It is a wretched and base-spirited thing that can conceive no honourable thoughts of God, but thinks him only like itself. But with faith, which is the well-pleasing ingredient of prayer, the lower thoughts a man has of himself, the higher and more honourably it makes him conceive of God. 'For my thoughts are not your thoughts, neither are your ways my ways', but as far above as the heavens are above the earth (*Isa.* 55:8).

This is the rule of a believing soul's conceiving of God, and expecting from him. And when a soul is thus placed on God, by trusting and believing in him, it is fixed: 'His heart is fixed, trusting in the LORD' (*Psa.* 112:7).

Oh, how wavering and inconstant is a soul, till it is fixed by this anchor, upon the ground of his immutable promises! It is tossed up and down with every wind, it is double-minded; now one way, then another; now in one mind, and shortly changed. And indeed, the soul is like the sea, capable of the least or greatest commotion (*James* 1:6–8).

I know not any thing that will either fix your hearts from wandering in prayer, or establish your hearts from trouble and disquiet after it, nothing that will so unburden and ease your spirits of care as this – to lay hold on God as all-sufficient, and lay this constraint on your hearts, to wait on him and his pleasure, to cast your souls on his promises that are so full and so free, and abide there, as at your anchorage point, in all the vicissitudes and changes of outward or inward things.

In *spiritual things* that concern your salvation, in that which is absolutely necessary, you may take the boldness to be absolute in it and say as Job, 'Though he slay me, yet will I trust in him'; and as Jacob, 'I will not let thee go, except thou bless me.' But in *outward things*, that have some usefulness in them, but are not always fitted for our chiefest good; or in the *degrees of spiritual gifts, and measures of graces*, the Lord calls us, without anxiety, to pour out our hearts in them unto him. But we should do it with submission to his pleasure, because he knows best what is best for us. In these, we are not bound to be confident to receive the particular we ask, but rather our confidence should pitch upon his good-will and favour, that he will certainly deny nothing that himself knows is good for us. And so in these we should absolutely cast ourselves without carefulness upon his loving and fatherly providence, and resign ourselves to him, to be disposed of in them as he sees convenient.

There is sometimes too much limitation of God and peremptoriness used with him in such things, in which his wisdom craves a latitude both in public and private matters, even as men's affections and interests are engaged; but ordinarily it is attended and followed with shame and disappointment in the end. And there is, on the other hand, intolerable remissness and slackness in many in pressing even the weightiest petitions of salvation, mortification, etc. This certainly arises from the diffidence and unbelief of the heart and the want of that rooted persuasion, both of the incomparable necessity and worth of the things themselves, and of his willingness and engagement to bestow them.

The word is doubled here, *Abba, Father,* the Syriac and Greek words signifying one thing, expressing the tender affection and love of God towards them that come to him: 'He that cometh to God must believe that he is, and that he is a rewarder of them that diligently seek him'; so he that comes to God must believe that he has the bowels and compassion of a Father and will be more easily inclined with our importunate cries than the fathers of our flesh. He may suffer his children to cry long, but it is not because he will not hear, but because he would hear them longer, and delights to hear their cry oftener. If he delays it is his wisdom to raise the value of his mercies and endear them to us, and to teach us to press our petitions, and plead for an answer.

Besides, this is much for our comfort that, from whomsoever, and whatsoever corner in the world, prayers come up to him, they cannot lack acceptance. All languages, all countries, all places are sanctified by Jesus Christ, that whosoever calls upon the name of the Lord, even from the ends of the earth, shall be saved. And truly it is a sweet meditation, to think that from *the ends of the earth* the cries of souls are heard, and that the *end* is as near heaven as the *middle*; and a wilderness as near as a paradise; that though we do not understand one another, yet we have one loving and living Father that understands all our meanings. And so the different languages and dialects of the members of this body make no confusion in heaven but meet together in his heart and affection, and are one perfume, one incense, sent up from the whole catholic church, which here is scattered on the earth. Oh, that the Lord would persuade us to cry in this way to our Father, in all our necessities!